CORVETTE
THE COMPLETE STORY
BY TIMOTHY K. TILTON

FIRST EDITION

FIRST PRINTING

Copyright © 1984 by TAB BOOKS Inc.

Printed in the United States of America

Reproduction or publication of the content in any manner, without express permission of the publisher, is prohibited. No liability is assumed with respect to the use of the information herein.

Library of Congress Cataloging in Publication data

Tilton, Timothy K.
   Corvette: the complete story.

   Includes index.
   1. Corvette automobile. I. Title.
TL215.C6T55   1984   629.2'222   84-8713
ISBN 0-8306-2107-5 (pbk.)

Cover photograph courtesy of Chevrolet Motor Division—General Motors Corporation.

Chapter opening drawings by Peachi Davis

Contents

	Introduction	v
1	**Corvette History and Development**	1
	Number One Rolls off the Line—Second Generation Arrives—Mako Shark Signals Third Generation—Fourth-Generation Corvette	
2	**Data, Details, and Notes**	36
	1953—1954—1955—1956—1957—1958—1959—1960—1961—1962—1963—1964—1965—1966—1967—1968—1969—1970—1971—1972—1973—1974—1975—1976—1977—1978—1979—1980—1981—1982—1983—1984	
3	**Corvette Fuel Injection Systems**	134
	Operation—Routine Maintenance and Adjustments—Service Operations—Throttle Body Injection for 1982	
4	**Corvette Disc Brakes**	167
	Disc Brake Problems—Disc Brake Solutions—Parking Brake Solutions	
5	**Corvette Restoration Techniques**	173
	Restoration Methodology—Corvette Restoration by General Motors	
6	**Corvette Fiberglass Repair and Repainting**	193
	Repair Procedures—Equipment Selection for Refinishing—Painting Methods and Techniques—Color Sanding and Compounding—Soft Bumper Refinishing—Refinishing Problems	
	Index	214

Introduction

There are few automobiles, past or present, that have the ability to command and generate such high levels of enthusiasm as the Chevrolet Corvette. Through a vast array of complex attitudes and intermingled emotions there has emerged a true Corvette mystique.

The roots of this mystique were born out of pure American ingenuity and postwar technology, with the Corvette soon rising to become the vanguard of General Motors advanced engineering, research, and design development departments. Through its main sales attractions—notably performance and image—the Corvette has continued to grow and successfully lead as North America's first mass-produced sports car.

One of the many problems enthusiasts and restorers experience when gathering information about any particular marque, such as the Corvette, is that this information seems to be scattered about in an almost endless variety of sources. Rarely does one find a wide variety of material in one resource.

What I have attempted to do in this volume is produce a handbook that presents the basic knowledge required for the enthusiast to enjoy his Corvette, while providing additional accurate information for the individual who is concerned with Corvette restoration.

While some of this Corvette history, and statistical and restoration information has been presented in other sources, nowhere has it all appeared in one single reference. In fact, many of the early historical facts have only appeared in relatively obscure publications; thus, for many of you, these facts will seem heretofore-unrevealed information.

This, then, leads us to the severest problem facing the automotive historian: the reconstruction of events through scattered bits and pieces of information. I don't know if anyone really knows—or ever *will* know—all the details surrounding the birth of the Corvette, but I am certain that what is presented here is the best available knowledge at this time.

I hope you will find the information contained herein both entertaining and informative, enabling you to enjoy your Corvette to its maximum potential.

Chapter 1

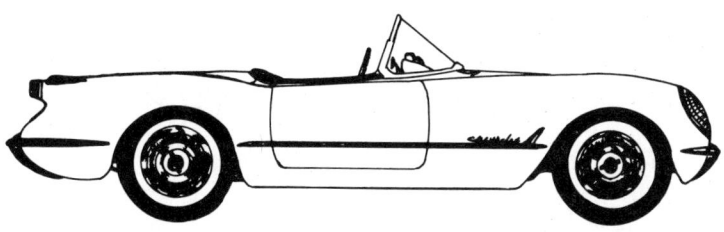

Corvette History and Development

Although many different types of materials have been used in automobiles throughout their history, the concept of using glass-reinforced plastic—commonly called fiberglass—for auto body construction has its heritage intertwined with two major wars. During World War II it became necessary to develop a material that was non-metallic to be used in the manufacture of American minesweepers. The new material, generated out of American ingenuity and wartime technology, was used with excellent results. Later, using this early pioneer work undertaken by Henry Kaiser and Owen-Corning, several prototype automobile bodies were constructed in 1944 with this new glass-reinforced plastic material.

Little development occurred after WWII. However, during 1951, the escalation of the Korean conflict sent a chilling message to the federal government that spelled rationing—and while steel was not as yet on the list of items that were placed under sales restrictions, there was some concern in Detroit. It became apparent to some that alternative materials should be considered for use in the construction of automobile bodies.

By sheer coincidence, the 1951 Motorama Auto Show in Los Angeles highlighted three cars featuring fiberglass bodies. One, designed and constructed by Bill Tritt, was a reconstructed, re-bodied Jeep, and was on display at the *Motor Trend* booth. Later, in February, *Life* magazine ran a story entitled "Plastic Bodies for Autos" that detailed the Glasspan Company's work with fiberglass for auto construction and featured Tritt's car, now renamed Alembic I.

Tritt's car and work by the Glasspan Company obviously caused an impression at GM, since they set up a private showing for the GM styling crew. Harley Earl, head of GM styling at the time, had already been working on a similar rebody project, that being a full-size 1952 Chevrolet convertible constructed with an all-fiberglass body. Although damaged in a rollover accident at the General Motors Proving Grounds late in 1953, this car paved the way for the Corvette project.

After gathering sufficient information—including that from Tritt's car and the 1952 fiberglass convertible—Harley Earl decided to accelerate the project. As part of this acceleration, Earl brought to the project Robert F. McLean, a design engineer, and gave him license to develop the new model's mechanical format. Through the efforts of the existing styling and engineering staffs at GM, a full-size plaster mockup was created by late April 1952.

The first person to view the plaster mockup (with the exception of the personnel working on the project) was Ed Cole, Chief of Chevrolet Engineering. After viewing the mockup in late April, Cole immediately liked the car and emphatically put his backing on the project with a promise of complete support.

After this initial screening came a formal presentation of GM management, members of which included Harlow Curtice, GM President; Thomas H. Keating, Chevrolet General Manager, and a number of other top management officials. This showing, which featured a further refinement of the model Cole had been shown, received the response Harley Earl was hoping for: authorization as Chevrolet's next entry on the Motorama Auto Show circuit.

The immediate problem to overcome was that of creating a rolling chassis. In those days, cars designed for the Motorama Auto Show circuit were not just styling exercises, but actual working models (Fig. 1-1). The target date for the introduction of the Motorama Corvette to the public was January 17, 1953, at the Waldorf-Astoria Hotel in New York City. On June 2, 1952, Maurice Olley, head of Chevrolet's Research and Development Department, was first shown a full-size plaster mockup of the car and asked to produce a chassis—in Olley's words, "... a chassis [of] a sports car, using components of known reliability, with adequate performance, a comfortable ride, and stable handling qualities ... "

The car was completed in time for the Manhattan Motorama and the resulting response was simply overwhelming (Fig. 1-2).

Fig. 1-1. Equipped with the Blue Flame six and Powerglide, the Corvette Nomad station wagon was only a prototype. The roofline and Nomad name did, however, show up in the Chevrolet lineup in 1955.

Crowds lined up for as much as 45 minutes just to catch a glimpse of Chevrolet's entry into the world of the sports car. GM made it a practice during these Motorama shows to query the showgoers with surveys in order to monitor their likes and dislikes. A number of the questions were directly related to the Corvette, such as, "How do you feel about using fiberglass as an auto body building material?" Overall response, as indicated by the Manhattan crowd to the new

Fig. 1-2. The EX-122 Motorama Corvette was first exhibited at the Waldorf-Astoria Hotel, January 14, 1953. Note the direction of the "wing" on the side trim and the Corvette script beneath the hood emblem.

car, was much better than expected with many respondants indicating that they would like to own the new Corvette. Armed with these enthusiastic survey results and such positive public response, Ed Cole approached Chevrolet General Manager Keating and urged him to put the now-popular two-seater into production.

Although the original Corvette prototypes had been constructed of fiberglass, initial plans at Chevrolet were developed to construct the car in a conventional manner out of sheetmetal. Since it was felt that the Corvette would only be a limited production sports car, the engineers planned on using Kirksite dies to press out the sheetmetal panels. These dies, unlike conventional steel dies, are quick to tool and cost relatively little. Their main drawback is that they have a short life expectancy, but this is acceptable if the car you produce will always be limited in numbers.

After subsequent study, the Kirksite plans were dropped and the chosen medium for production became fiberglass. Chevrolet asked private industry as well as other GM corporate divisions for bids on the construction of 12,300 complete sets of body components. Fisher Body Division sent in the high bid; Molded Fiber Glass Company of Ashtabula, Ohio, headed by Robert S. Morrison, sent in the low bid. It wasn't long before Morrison was asked to come to Detroit to discuss his participation in the Corvette project.

Morrison had several meetings with Chevrolet's top executives, including Carl Jakust, Chevrolet's chief body engineer, and Jim Premo, project engineer, as plans were being finalized for production. Everything seemed set to go until Morrison came to Detroit to meet with the Chevrolet purchasing agent and the project buyer. When Morrison arrived he was surprised to find them gone; his appointment had not been canceled until that moment. As Morrison was about to leave, Elmer Gormeson, Chevrolet's director of purchases, stepped out and said, "Bob, have you got a minute?"

It was at this very moment that Morrison discovered that, on the previous day, a high-level management meeting between GM and Chevrolet had been held and the decision to go with an all-metal body had again been made. It now appeared that the purchasing agent and project buyer were out frantically looking for sources of steel body parts! The fate of the Corvette body as we know it today came down to that chance meeting of Morrison and Gormeson. Morrison was finally able to convince Chevrolet that fiberglass was indeed the material to use and that his company had the ability to produce the number and quality of fiberglass parts required. Years later Morrison stated, "I feel quite certain if I hadn't bumped into him in front of that elevator, there would not be a fiberglass plastic body on the Corvette."

Due to the size of the contract from Chevrolet, Morrison established a new Molded Fiber Glass Body Company plant in Ashtabula, Ohio. Since Chevrolet wanted to go into production as soon as possible, there was not enough time to proceed with the preferred method of using matched metal dies. Instead, the initial body parts were formed by the vacuum-bag method, using wooden or plaster molds. During the time required for the machining of the matched metal molds, Morrison subcontracted with the Lunn Laminate Company to mold the first Corvette body parts by this method. In all, the entire production run of 1953 models and some 1954 models—approximately 1000 cars—were constructed by the vacuum-bag method.

NUMBER ONE ROLLS OFF THE LINE

Molded fiberglass body parts, after construction in Ashtabula, were shipped to the assembly plant in Flint, Michigan. This first assembly plant was originally an old Chevrolet Customer Delivery garage located at Van Slyke and Atherton Road. Initial production of the 1953 models began sometime around mid-June with the first production Corvette, serial number E53F001001, rolling off the assembly line on Wednesday, June 30, 1953 (Fig. 1-3). The rate of

Fig. 1-3. Corvette Number One comes off the line at the Flint, Michigan assembly line June 30, 1953. Driving No. 001 is Tony Kleiber, with general manager of GM assembly plants R.G. Ford in the middle and Flint plant manager F.J. Fessenden.

Fig. 1-4. Nine cars were gathered for the press to observe on June 30, 1953. Journalists would not be permitted behind the wheel of the new sports car at the Milford high bank test track until September 29. This kept road tests out of magazines until later in the year.

Corvette assembly was fairly low at first—probably only one car per day—due primarily to the lack of experience and know-how required for the new type of body material, along with problems associated with new line startup. The rate of assembly soon accelerated to approximately three cars per day, and finally to six cars per day under full plant production.

The exact date on which the last 1953 model was constructed is not known, but since it appears that the 289th Corvette was completed by December 21st, presumably the last model, E53F001300, was finished before Christmas. In all, the first year's production total ran to 300 from the Flint plant.

In a press release dated June 30, 1953, Chevrolet Motor Division announced the release of the first Corvette off the assembly line and predicted the 1953 assembly rate of 50 per month (Fig. 1-4). Chevrolet even enthusiastically predicted " . . . 1000 plastic bodies a month for the 1954 production of the Corvette." These models were to be produced at the new assembly plant located in St. Louis, Missouri.

By December of 1953 the St. Louis plant was already in operation and had produced either 14 or 15 cars (the exact number is not recorded). Although actually produced in 1953, these cars were definitely 1954 models as indicated by their VIN (Vehicle Identification Number) numbers beginning with E54 and the "S" stamp denoting construction at the St. Louis plant.

Press releases were available for newspaper and magazine publication beginning prior to overall production in 1953, but press access to the new Corvettes in the form of official observation and driving analysis was not granted until Sept. 29, 1953, at the GM proving grounds in Milford, Michigan. With magazine lead time being several months, this meant that reports could not appear before December. By the time the 300th Corvette had been built, only 183 had actually been sold.

Even with good reviews of the new model, lagging sales continued through the 1954 model year (Fig. 1-5). More road tests

Fig. 1-5. The 1954 Motorama saw the Corvette roadster, now a production car, and two dream cars. Behind the hardtop '54 Corvette is the fastback Corvair; the name survived, the car did not. In the rear is a fiberglass Nomad Corvette station wagon.

and reviews appeared, the majority of them giving excellent test marks in all areas except performance. This factor—lack of performance—coupled with General Motor's bad press timing and the rumors of Ford's new two-seater sports car (the Thunderbird) reduced the anticipated 12,000 car sales projection for 1954 to an actual production total of 3639. In fact, by January 1, 1955, Chevrolet still had a backlog of 1076 unsold 1954 Corvettes. Clearly, the future of the Corvette was in jeopardy (Fig. 1-6).

With such a large holdover of cars from the previous year, production was trimmed to only 700 for the 1955 model year. This occurred despite the introduction of the optional 265 cubic-inch V-8 engine (Fig. 1-7). Meanwhile, the competition in the form of Ford's Thunderbird sold 16,155 cars in 1955—almost 23 times the sales volume of the Corvette. It was only the sheer confidence held by Ed Cole and a small group of supporters that was able to stay the decision to drop the Corvette from Chevrolet's production lineup (Fig. 1-8).

With the Corvette having narrowly received a stay of execution, it was obvious that something was needed to get the car off the ground. That something was named Zora Arkus-Duntov. Hired in May of 1953 and destined for the research and development department, Duntov soon moved over to the Corvette project, where he was responsible for all facets of design except body fabrication.

Fig. 1-6. Early '53-55 Corvette dashboards were extremely simple. Note the location of the tachometer. Later models would find it located beneath the speedometer, closer to the driver's line of vision.

Fig. 1-7. The large V in the side script denotes a V-8 engine in this 1955 Corvette. Virtually all '55 models had this optional engine with the exception of approximately ten cars which received the Blue Flame Six.

Fig. 1-8. Many organized events are held throughout the year for the Corvette enthusiast. Three main sanctioning bodies cover the U.S. and Canada—The National Council of Corvette Clubs, Inc.; Western States Corvette Council, Inc.; and the Canadian Council of Corvette Clubs.

Duntov's first involvement with the Corvette came with the reworking of the suspension in order to improve the handling for the 1956 and 1957 models. These chassis improvements, in addition to a refined body with removable hardtop, power softtop, and roll-up windows, all added to the car's desirability. He also gave the Corvette its first association with performance by overseeing a low-budget racing team of three cars. This team traveled to Daytona Beach for the annual Speed Week, where the new performance-minded Corvettes established runs in excess of 150 mph (Fig. 1-9).

The attitude at Chevrolet from the start was that of sink-or-swim for the Corvette. Relatively few changes had been made during the first three years of production and it came down to the 1956 model with its subtle improvements to decide the Corvette's fate. Duntov and his engineers must have struck the proper chords

Fig. 1-9. Fuel injection for 1957 boasted one horsepower per cubic inch. The 283-hp RPO 579 option cost $450 and was well worth it. This engine has the correct air cleaner.

Fig. 1-10. New figures compiled by the National Corvette Restorers Society indicate that over 1000 Corvettes in 1957 came equipped with RPO 579 Ramjet fuel injection.

with the public, as sales jumped to 4012 in 1956.

The single most significant innovation of the 1957 Corvette was the introduction of its high performance Rochester Ramjet Fuel injection. With the advent of this new induction system, a major milestone was established of one horsepower for every cubic inch—the first time ever for a mass-produced American production engine (Fig. 1-10).

America was beginning to become performance-minded and the way to get the public's attention was by racing—and winning. The first race of the 1957 season was in New Smyrna, Florida, where Paul Goldsmith handily won over a large field of production Jaguar XK 140s, Mercedes 300 SL series, and Ford Thunderbirds.

One of the year's most prestigious races, the Nassau Trophy Race, was held during Nassau Speed Week later that year. Only 26 of the starting 47 entries finished the race, with all four Corvettes entered going strong at the end. They placed first, second, third, and fourth.

The fuel injection option was indicative of the stance Chevrolet and Duntov were taking toward producing a serious performance-minded sports car, one that would compete on equal footing with its European competition (Fig. 1-11).

Other options indicated this serious attitude at Chevrolet. A

Fig. 1-11. Corvette for 1957 saw major performance options. In addition to dual four-bbl carburetors, Chevrolet included Ramjet fuel injection, heavy-duty brakes and suspension, limited slip differential, and a four-speed close-ratio transmission.

heavy-duty racing suspension (RPO 684) was offered for $725; it consisted of a quick-steering adapter, Positraction, heavier leaf springs, larger, stiffer shocks, front anti-sway bar and heavier springs, and ceramic-metallic brake linings with finned and ventilated drums. This was also the first year the Borg-Warner T-10 four-speed transmission was made available. Corvette sales were increasing every year; 1955 saw only 1700 produced while 1956 more than doubled that figure to 4467. High performance brought the 1957 sales figures up to 6339. Sales jumped to 9168 for the 1958 production model. In only four short years, Corvette sales had increased approximately 540 percent.

Although General Motors joined the Automotive Manufacturer's Association in early 1957 in a resolution against any auto industry support for racing, the options list did not seem to reflect this policy. The heavy-duty suspension along with four optional engines and four-speed transmission were available on all Corvettes well into the '60s (Fig. 1-12).

Styling had progressed steadily, if slowly, from 1957. Quad headlights offered in 1958 were carried through and became standard. Louvers on the 1958 hood were gone by 1959 but it was not until 1961—actually a mild facelift of the 58-60 models—that there appeared a hint of what was to come in Corvette's second generation.

The force behind these styling changes was Bill Mitchell. He relieved Harley Earl as chief of GM Design and created styling exercises beginning with the XP-700 (Fig. 1-13). The rear end previewed on that showcar was a glimpse of what was to be in 1961

Fig. 1-12. Fuel injection began in 1957 and continued for eight years.

and 1962, while his racing Sting Ray was a look at the soon-to-come second generation Corvette.

The chassis for the Sting Ray racer was actually from the Corvette SS race car, designed for competition at Sebring and built in 1957 (Fig. 1-14). After the AMA ban in '57, the car went into

Fig. 1-13. Bill Mitchell took over from Harley Earl as chief of GM Design and created the XP-700 in 1960. It featured, among other items, the ducktailed rear end that would be carried over into later models.

Fig. 1-14. Bill Mitchell's racing Sting Ray, a predecessor to the second major body change in the Corvette lineage. Note the Corvette badge on the hood and "Stingray" above the exhaust header.

storage. The resurrected chassis was mated to Mitchell's body design in 1959 and raced during the 1959 and 1960 seasons, frequently by Dr. Dick Thompson. Few knew of GM's involvement in the project or the fact that the car was the rebodied SS racer. Fewer yet knew that this shape, along with the Shark XP-755, built in 1961, was the forebear of the next generation of Corvettes (Fig. 1-15).

Fig. 1-15. Built in 1961, the Shark XP-755 was the forerunner of the Sting Ray series beginning with the 1963 models.

SECOND GENERATION ARRIVES

The Corvette had gone through many major changes in its ten-year history, but the single greatest change—both visual and mechanical to that date—was to greet the public for the 1963 model year. Styling, of course, came under the direct supervision of William Mitchell and utilized his design; the mechanical engineering was headed by Zora Arkus-Duntov.

Chevrolet actually began in earnest to work on the radical new Corvette in mid-1960. Stylists were given the go-ahead to create designs based on the early Mitchell race car. Many full-scale models and sketches, along with experimental cars such as the XP-755, were involved before finally arriving at the finished design (Fig. 1-16). In the end, the new Corvette Sting Ray bore an amazing resemblance to its racing Sting Ray predecessor. Concerning the new Corvette, Chevrolet Styling said: "The new Corvette was to be a broad-shouldered, masculine, American sports car. The lines were to be clean, with just enough detail to keep the styling value high in the eyes of the public."

In addition to an all-new facelift, the Corvette received a new model as well, the coupe (Fig. 1-17). The sleek fastback was perhaps the most visually exciting of the two new styles. Among the Mitchell stylists, other body designs had also been contemplated. Serious thought, favored by Ed Cole, was given to a four-passenger version, but this was opposed by both Mitchell and Duntov as being out of character and a compromise of the Corvette's distinction and personality. A two-plus-two coupe, similar to the concept embodied by the two plus two Jaguar, was actually carried out with a full-size

Fig. 1-16. It's not a Dual-Ghia or a Studebaker, but another design exercise on the second generation Corvette. This is the 1963 Rondine.

Fig. 1-17. Prior to 1963, a Corvette was just a Corvette but now it was a Sting Ray! Everything was changed on this second generation Vette except the powertrain. The 1963 model marked the emergence of a sophisticated GT machine.

mockup before it was quietly forgotten.

New fixtures and equipment necessary for production were brought to the St. Louis plant, along with teams of engineers and technicians. With the body panels arriving from a plant in Ohio, initial fabrication could begin on pilot production of the second-generation Corvette. During this familiarization period, 25 cars were scheduled for production to be used for press showings and public previews.

Although initial preproduction construction of the new designs had gone well, Chevrolet was hesitant to announce the availability date of the coupe and roadster. *Motor Trend* reported in its October 1962 issue that the coupe might not be available until a 1963 introduction date. Since magazines typically have a three-month lead time, the article probably was written around August, but by the end of September, 675 new Corvettes had been built with the number shooting to over 2000 in October (Fig. 1-18).

Demand for the new second-generation Corvettes necessitated the addition of a second shift at the St. Louis plant, the first production demand of its type for Corvette. It was not unusual to encounter 60-day waiting periods for the new models, with little or no opportunity to deal on the price. If you wanted one, you had to get in line and pay the price!

The Corvette for '63 was an entirely new automobile, not just a warmed-over styling exercise. Duntov states the design parameters were to include a fully independent suspension, frame-mounted differential, high power-to-weight ratio, and a newly designed frame. Chevrolet wanted the frame-mounted differential with fully independent suspension for good handling and ride as well as to preserve their engine/transmission combinations.

The design was a package concept. The best possible arrangement to achieve good ride and superb handling for two people, in addition to certain fixed parameters such as engine and transmission placement, fuel tank location, suspension, etc., was achieved by interpreting this data through a series of programs.

An example of component selection and component location involves the rear axle and differential. Duntov felt that he had three choices: live axle, De Dion with swing axles, or fully independent. Although Chevrolet engineers already had experience with the De Dion system on the Corvette SS race car that appeared at Sebring in 1957, it simply took up too much room. For this reason—and the out-and-out rejection of a live axle—Duntov opted for the fully-independent system. The basis for the independent system came from the CERV-1 research car which was fitted with a three-link design. The major difference between the CERV-1 design and the final production design was the substitution of a transverse leaf spring instead of coil springs.

The basic IRS system has been used since its production car debut in 1963, and continues to be used today with few modifications. It works extremely well. The rear wheels with special spindles are suspended in radius arms that extend rearward from the attachment point on the frame ahead of the rear wheels. This arrangement controls fore-and-aft wheel movement. Lateral con-

Fig. 1-18. Lighter than previous Corvettes but structurally more rigid, the new 1963 Sting Rays were available in the traditional roadster and the all-new fastback coupe.

trol of the wheels is handled by two lateral control rods and two double universal-jointed axle shafts. This design of wheel spindle attachment controls the side and fore-and-aft movement of each wheel.

This unique arrangement clearly has numerous advantages, including eliminating completely torque steer and tramp, allowing the outside tire to remain merely vertical during extreme cornering and loading, and, finally, providing for an outstanding ride.

In addition to the new rear suspension, the Corvette also received an entirely new, highly strengthened frame and a new spherical-joint front suspension (replacing outmoded kingpins).

Besides the coupe and roadster, a third model was designed as an answer to Carrol Shelby's Ford Cobras. Although exact details have been lost to history, it appears that 1000 special Sting Rays, known as the Corvette Gran Sport, were to be built. Unfortunately, General Motors clamped the lid on overt racing activities and the project ground to a halt, but not before five prototypes had been constructed—two roadsters and three coupes, (Fig. 1-19).

Although the Gran Sport resembled the 1963 Sting Ray, it had numerous features that made it substantially different. First of all, it was 1200 pounds lighter than a standard production model. This was due primarily to the use of large-diameter steel tubing for the frame and a body thickness about half that of a normal Sting Ray. Aluminum was also used throughout the car wherever possible, along with light alloy components. Total body weight (including doors, windows, and hood) was approximately 375 pounds. With the aluminum 377-cubic inch engine and the car race-ready, the Corvette GS tipped the scales at 1995 pounds wet.

Fig. 1-19. Fuel injection for 1963 saw a new, more efficient air intake system.

The period between 1964 and 1967 was actually one of refinement for the Corvette. Minor cosmetic changes accompanied major engine changes, with many Corvette enthusiasts feeling that the '67 was the best year built.

As explained in detail later in the section on bodywork, Chevrolet did not actually build the molded fiberglass parts, but subcontracted them from (principally) the Molded Fiber Glass Products company. Molded fiberglass panels were delivered to the St. Louis plant, assembled into bodies, and dropped on the assembly line at the appropriate spot. What is not so well known is that during the period from January 1964 through 1967, Corvette bodies were also subcontracted from another non-GM company, Mitchell-Bentley Corp., a subsidiary of the A.O. Smith Corporation in Ionia, Michigan.

With a strike for the first time at Chevrolet in 1964, painted and trimmed units came from Ionia to the Corvette plant at St. Louis, ready to drop in at the same point as the St. Louis-built bodies. Although these bodies were used as early as January 1964, no prefix is used in conjunction with the serial number to differentiate between Chevrolet-St. Louis and A.O. Smith-Ionia bodies. Effective with Corvette number 109678, the body source is identified by prefixing the serial number with the letter "S" for St. Louis and "A" for A.O. Smith.

It soon became apparent that the new coupe design, along with the distinctive Sting Ray styling, was a boon to Corvette sales. From an all-time sales high of nearly 11,000 in 1961, the production run for 1964 easily exceeded 22,000—a doubling of sales in merely three years.

Highlights of refinements during the 1964-67 period include removal of the rear window divider and functional side vents in 1964, caliper-type disc brakes, and the 396-cubic inch, 425-horsepower "porcupine" engine in 1965. The 427-cubic inch engine followed in 1966 and 1967. Of course, numerous small changes were made throughout this period, almost all of them for the better. One change not especially welcomed was the deletion of the optional Ramjet fuel injection for the 327 engine at the end of the 1965 model year.

MAKO SHARK SIGNALS THIRD GENERATION

The second generation Corvette, 1963-1967, has been the most short-lived design in the four-generation history of the marque (not including the latest design released in 1983). The reason only

120,000 or so second-generation Corvettes saw production is that near the end of 1963, William Mitchell gave Larry Shinoda the assignment of creating a spinoff of the Shark showcar. Shinoda came up with the Mako Shark II, which would eventually inspire the 1968 and later third-generation Corvettes. The radical Mako Shark II was first revealed in April 1965 and made the circuit of all the major international auto shows (Fig. 1-20). Although Shinoda created the initial design, the final styling work was completed by Chevrolet's chief stylist, David Holls.

The new design was actually intended for the 1967 model year, but problems with air drag proved to be considerably greater than expected. It was Duntov who convinced General Manager "Pete" Estes to push the introduction of the new design back to 1968 while wind tunnel tests and design refinements could be made. Prior wind tunnel testing had indicated that unusually high amounts of lift were being experienced at the front of the car, decreasing forward vision and maneuvering capability. The rear of the car was aerodynamically clean; only the front of the car required additional development.

At first the third-generation Corvette was somewhat slow to catch on (Fig. 1-21). During its initial introduction, sales for the 1968 model year set a mild record of 28,566 units, up from 22,940 in 1967. By the time the 1969 model year ended, the new Stingray

Fig. 1-20. The Mako Shark II, designed by David Holls, was built in 1967 for the 1967 production year. Duntov convinced "Pete" Estes, GM general manager, to wait a year so further testing could be completed before the third generation Corvette was released.

Fig. 1-21. The third generation of Corvettes appeared in 1968. The completely new and aerodynamic body gave Corvette a look that would continue until 1982.

(note spelling) set a truly impressive record of 38,762 units, nearly a 26.3 percent increase! (It should be mentioned, though, that Chevrolet prolonged the production of the 1969 model due to an early-year strike; this helped account for the record figure.)

The 1970 model wasn't introduced to the public until late February of that year. Only minor changes in trim and lighting separated it from its predecessor. This was the year, however, of the big engine. Chevrolet had pumped the 427-cubic inch engine to 454 cubes. This did not reflect a desire for more horsepower, but rather an answer to the increasingly stringent Federal emission controls. The 454 actually developed *less* power than its 427 forerunner.

This was the beginning of the end of the "power years." Although the big-block 454 was offered through 1974, it never reached its maximum potential as engines had in the past.

Along with federal regulations, a change in the nature of the Corvette owner also occurred. This is reflected in the availability of cut-pile carpeting, leather trim, tinted glass, and air conditioning (the latter of which was found in over half of the 1970 production run). The ground-thundering sports car developed by Duntov was slowly changing into a luxury sports GT (Fig. 1-22).

The big news for 1974 was a severe reduction in compression ratio in all engine sizes; this reduced drastically both horsepower and torque, and forewarned the direction of engine development to

Fig. 1-22. Factory standard leather seats, electric windows, automatic transmission, tilt steering wheel, and a plethora of comfort options made the modern Corvette a true GT tourer.

come in subsequent years. The base L-48 engine was reduced in horsepower from 300 to 270, while the LS-5 option sank from 390 to 365. Styling changes in 1971 and 1972 were again very subtle, with the next visual change occurring in 1973 (Fig. 1-23).

Federal mandates in 1973 demanded bumpers that could survive a 5-mph front-end barrier crash. Gone was the Corvette's lean, hard look, replaced by a urethane pad covering the impact-

Fig. 1-23. The XP-882 was originally designed using a pair of two-rotor engines combining to form a four-rotor, 420-bhp engine. First shown in 1973, the car later hit the auto show circuit renamed the Aero-Vette. It then was powered with a 400-c.i. small-block Chevrolet engine.

absorption equipment. The same treatment for the rear would not appear until the 1974 models. It soon became apparent to Chevrolet that they were on the proper course with the GT styling of the Corvette. Production for 1973 came close to 34,500 models, with at least 8000 customers' orders returned at the end of the 1973 model year.

Changes from 1973 through the next four model years were kept to a minimum. The most noteworthy changes were actually *deletions,* such as the disappearance of the convertible from the 1976

Fig. 1-24. The XP-987GT was designed by GM with coachwork by Pinninfarina. The car was built on a shortened 914 chassis using that suspension and braking system coupled to a two-rotor Wankel engine. It first appeared at the Frankfurt Auto show, September, 1973. This car is commonly called the Corvette two-rotor.

lineup. The now-familiar tunnelback roof design, reminiscent of the Ferrari GTO and Porsche 904, was also changed at the end of the '77 production year (Fig. 1-24).

It had taken 16 years for Corvette to sell 250,000 models, this occurring in 1969. Just eight years later, in 1977, the third-generation Corvette had the distinction of rolling total sales up to 500,000 units. Chevrolet general manager Robert D. Lund drove the half-millionth Corvette, priced at $11,455.45, off the assembly line in St. Louis on March 15, 1977.

The Corvette's silver anniversary year, 1978, was celebrated with a significant styling modification and two limited-production models. The tunnelback rear roof design was retailored into a large glassback—a fastback window with wraparound sides. Two special editions were available. The Silver Anniversary model featured a silver over gray lower body two-tone paint scheme, alloy wheels with Goodyear GT radial tires, tinted glass lift-off roof panels, and color-keyed interior. An Official Pace Car, similar to that displayed and driven at Indianapolis, featured a silver metallic lower body topped by a black upper body paint treatment, alloy wheels with wide tires, front and rear air spoilers, and "Pace Car" decals (Fig. 1-25). (An interesting feature found only on the Official Pace Car

Fig. 1-25. Following in the steps of its predecessors, the 1982 Corvette refined the styling design started in 1968. This was the last year for this body style.

Fig. 1-26. Forebears of four Corvette generations—the 1953, 1963, 1968, and 1984 models.

edition was the use of 1979-design bucket seats instead of the 1978 seats found on all other 1978 models. Many tried to imitate the Official Pace Car model only to be given away by the wrong seats!)

Front and rear spoilers were integrated into the 1980 facelift; the 1981 and 1982 versions were essentially the same, showing little outward change. The 1982 model officially ceased production on October 14, 1982, thus bringing to a close the series of third-generation Corvettes. A new, restyled model debuted in January 1983, heralding another generation of Corvettes (Fig. 1-26).

FOURTH-GENERATION CORVETTE

When General Motors asked the question, "How do you redesign a sports car that has held basically the same styling—and enjoyed tremendous popularity—since 1968?", they did not anticipate Jerry Palmer's answer. Palmer, chief stylist for Chevy Studio Three, the locked studio inside General Motor's Design Staff center, stated that you do it "With one eye on the past and one eye on the next century."

Even though the fourth-generation Corvette (Fig. 1-27) is years ahead of its competitors, it is interesting to note that early

Fig. 1-27. The all-new fourth generation 1984 Corvette.

"spy" photos of the model can actually be traced as far back as 1966. During this time William Mitchell was still vice-president in charge of design and he and his contemporaries produced the XP-819, using 327 V-8 mounted behind the rear wheels. As anyone who has watched a Porsche slide around a racetrack will tell you, putting the power behind the rear wheels produces tremendous amounts of oversteer.

Development continued with the Astro II showcar in 1968, this time with the engine in the mid-engine position. A sleeker design soon appeared in 1970, the XP-882; it was this model that began the first serious rumors of a new mid-engine Corvette. Further testing and design continued, resulting in the aluminum-bodied XP-895 and the XP-987GT. The latter showcar was designed using the then-radical two-rotor Wankel rotary engine, to which GM had purchased the manufacturing rights. While only one step in the development of the new Corvette, several features from the XP-987GT did find incorporation into latter GM cars, notably the headlight configuration and the front air dam.

During the 1973 Paris Auto Salon, two experimental showcars were displayed, the previously shown two-rotor Wankel-powered XP-987GT and a newly designed Duntov-inspired four-rotor Wankel-powered model. Duntov had two dual-rotor Wankel engines mated together and placed in the showcar. The four-rotor performed well as evidenced by GM's president Ed Cole running the needle up to 148 mph at the Milford test track.

The rotary engine soon fell from contention and the XP-987GT soon had a new engine—a 305-cubic inch V8 mounted transversely. Along with the new engine came a new name, the Corvette Aero, or simply the Aerovette. Although the gullwing doors and the steeply-raked windshield were not practical for production, the basic design of the futuristic car did provide the starting point for the fourth-generation Corvette.

Jerry Palmer began early at Chevrolet Exterior Three, where all of the Corvette design work has been initiated. He worked in conjunction with Chuck Jordan and under William Mitchell until Mitchell was replaced as vice-president of design by Irv Rybicki. It was sometime during 1978, with Rybicki at the helm and Dave McLellan as Corvette chief engineer, that the decision was made to stay with the front-engine configuration instead of a mid-engine placement. One reason for this was Chevrolet's desire to maintain the basic Corvette identity and Corvette "face." Even with its distinctive features, the newly designed Corvette still has a familiar resemblance to its predecessors.

Apparently the Aerovette (and perhaps many of its ancestors) were built to only ⅞ scale and this prevented the GM engineers from fitting it with all of the necessary components found on a standard Corvette—not to mention measuring interior room, engine compartment accessibility, and the like. Even when design projections were made increasing the experimental car to full scale, usable passenger space and engine compartment volume were lacking.

Early on in the creation of the new model (and, indeed, throughout the entire design process), full-size clays were compared side-by-side with what GM thought to be the fourth generation's contemporaries. The one car that GM used over and over again for comparison was the Ferrari 308 GTB. Full-size clays had been compared as early as November 1976.

The crucial test for the fourth-generation model occurred on Oct. 23, 1978. On this date a face-off took place between the mid-engined clay mockup, the front-engined design, a model of the 1980 Corvette, and the Ferrari 308 GTB. The comparison was held to determine which route to follow, front or mid-engine. As history recorded the event, we now know that the front engine design won out (Fig. 1-28).

From a practical standpoint, it also became clear that the historical configuration of the Corvette offered optimum packaging for its customers while still allowing for a new and exciting body style coupled with innovative engineering. Change for the sake of

Fig. 1-28. Although not a mid-engine design, Corvette's new chassis provides state-of-the-art features including unique "backbone" drivetrain with the engine and transmission rigidly attached to the differential by an aluminum C section beam.

change alone would not be sufficient; however, when the stylists created the clamshell hood for superior engine compartment accessibility, many underhood items were redesigned including the air cleaner, valve covers, fan shroud, sculptured T-handled dipstick, and a black-and-gray battery from Delco. At one point the engineers even held lengthy discussions concerning the eventual color of the high-tension cables leading to the spark plugs. When the final design package was approved, Jerry Palmer said, "We've designed a car without compromises."

With the basic engineering package decided upon and the "final" clay mockup approved, it now became the job of Palmer to refine the Corvette's new shape into an aerodynamically acceptable package. Although the basic shape had already been decided upon, only four points were actually physically fixed: seat clearance and headroom (defining roof height), front bumper height, upper windshield edge (for visibility), and lower windshield edge (ending just in back of the distributor). With the exception of these points, all other points could be modified if necessary.

Since GM's new multimillion dollar wind tunnel (which would have allowed full-scale testing) was not yet completed, smaller ⅓-scale clays were used for preliminary design testing at the Harrison Radiator cooling tunnel. Preliminary modifications were made, the most notable being the Kamm-style rear treatment with further full-scale testing to be held at the Lockheed wind tunnel in Atlanta, Georgia.

Full-scale testing finally indicated that the new Corvette was nearly a full 25 percent slipperier than its 1982 predecessor. Drag coefficient for the 1984 Corvette proved to be a slight 0.341 with the headlights down and 0.361 with them in the fully-opened position, compared to 0.44 for the '82 model.

All tests were conducted with the top on and the windows rolled up. With the body in stock form, total lift at front and rear is just slightly over 100 pounds at 100 mph. It should be obvious that little design work will be required to modify the body to produce down pressure sufficient for the racetrack or serious boulevard/ street racer/freeway flyer.

Although all the ramifications haven't been felt yet, all-out racers may be able to profit from Max Shenkel's work. Shenkel, a racing enthusiast, works on the GM Engineering staff and has constructed a 1/10-scale model competition Corvette in his off hours. Shenkel's model sports the typical race car modifications: body widened slightly, lowered, extended nose, air dam up front with a spoiler at the rear. Outboard exhaust and a large hood bulge, necessary for the inevitable racing induction system, complete the model.

Test results from Shenkel's work indicate the standard production Corvette body is very clean and efficient. With a low air dam in front and a high spoiler at the rear, impressive figures have been generated in the wind tunnel. Under complete race trim with 50mm air dam clearance and a 162mm high rear spoiler, over 200 pounds of negative lift (downforce) have been generated.

The 1984 Chevrolet Corvette officially went on sale to the public on Thursday, March 24, 1983, in the land of the automobile, California. The new Corvette was designated a 1984 model because it had been engineered to meet and surpass 1984 emissions, safety, and fuel economy standards. This careful blend of yesterday's styling and tomorrow's technology and sophistication provided *Motor Trend* magazine with the chance to say that the new Corvette is "... the best-handling production car in the world today, regardless of price."

Comparison to the 1982 third-generation Corvette showed that the new design is 1.1 inches lower, 8.8 inches shorter, and fully 2 inches wider, allowing for increased front and rear track and greater head, leg, and shoulder room. With all these dimensions reduced, weight is cut to 3192 pounds—down 175 pounds—allowing for better handling and maneuvering.

Standard features have made this latest model a Grand Touring machine and include air conditioning, electronically tuned AM/FM radio with digital clock, power windows, liquid crystal analog display, digital instrumentation, one-piece removable roof panel, electronic remote control sports mirrors, ergonomically designed and wool-padded high-contour bucket seats, leather-wrapped steering wheel, leather transmission shift-lever boot, advanced driver information system, load area security shade, power radio antenna, halogen headlamps and fog lamps, hatchback controlled by any of three remote electrical releases, and a built-in theft deterrent system.

One of the truest measures of a performance automobile is the examination of vehicle dynamics as expressed in lateral acceleration. Chevrolet measures it through a series of tests where the car accelerates through a 108-foot radius circle to the point where the tires just begin to lose adhesion with the road surface. Based on tests such as these at the GM Proving Grounds, Corvettes equipped with the Z51 Performance Handling Package have recorded lateral acceleration figures up to .95 Gs.

If you measure performance strictly by the time it takes to get from one end of a straight road to the other, then you will not be impressed with this latest Corvette. Laden with the latest federally imposed smog equipment and safety devices, the fourth-generation model turns in fairly respectable times of just under 15 seconds at around 90 mph for the quarter mile—really not all that bad when compared to the other competition around today. Top speed has been improved though, the increase due to the superior aerodynamics—estimates for the 48-state model are approximately 130-135 mph while the European export model is said to have 145 mph capability.

One of the major complaints in the recent past has been the quality of the Corvette's paint and finish. Most of these problems resulted from the color disparity between fiberglass and urethane compounds used for the bumpers, and the fact that micro-pits and strands of glass tended to stick out of the fiberglass and fiberglass panels, developing uneven surfaces at the bonding seams. These problems now have been solved through two techniques, the simplest being to place the junction of major panels along a natural body seam or break line. The second technique—not so simple—was to develop a new method of body construction. Essentially, the process involves an in-mold coating process. The proper amount of sheet molding compound (SMC) is put between the body dies and pressed at a pressure of 1000 psi and at a temperature of 300° until the desired shape is achieved. After a curing time, the dies are separated by .005-inch and liquid urethane is injected. After curing a second time, the panel is ready for painting.

Increased attention to road noise and vibration has resulted in added insulation of the passenger compartment with formed, acoustically backed carpeting and a liberal dosage of amberlite, urethane foam, and resinated materials.

Although not the most striking feature when the new Corvette is first viewed, the suspension is really one of the most impressive facets of the car. At the heart of the suspension is a new fully welded steel frame integrated with a birdcage structure that uses high-strength steel in strategic locations. Attached to this birdcage structure are the roof, door-sealing panels, dash, and sections of the undercarriage. Bolt-on stiffening braces reinforce the painted and galvanized structure. A bolt-on aluminum frame extension supports the rear bumper; a similar design is used up front. Both the extensions and bumpers are designed for easy replacement. In addition, a unique design approach involves the use of a U-shaped stamped aluminum channel beam to connect the rear of the transmission housing to the differential. The driveshaft runs inside this aluminum channeling.

Dave McLellan, Corvette's chief engineer, states, "Even in its standard suspension configuration, the new Corvette is a sports car absolutely superior to any production vehicle in its part of the market." Some of this superiority can be traced to the all-new five-link independent rear suspension that provides precise wheel control, reduction in lateral force compliance, and promotion of excellent understeer characteristics much like that of the front suspension design. Design features in front represent a major breakthrough in technology through the use of aluminum for the major front suspension components. Upper and lower control arms and knuckles along with the lateral control support arm in the rear are all constructed from aluminum.

Additional technology has been employed to eliminate the coil springs from the front suspension in an innovative manner by replacing them with a single transversely mounted fiberglass leaf spring. In fact, this newly designed leaf spring is found both front and rear. While these new springs feature a 50 percent weight reduction, they also feature a major improvement in durability. With steel springs, the typical full jounce extension is limited to approximately 75,000 cycles; the new fiberglass springs have been tested to 5,000,000 cycles without a failure.

In an effort to control roll stiffness, a 20mm stabilizer bar is standard with a 25mm bar included in the Performance Handling

Package option. An integral steering dampener is featured, which aids steering wheel feedback from irregular road surfaces. Combined with this is a relatively fast turning ratio of 15.5:1. A faster ratio is available under the Handling Package option. Other suspension highlights include lifelong stabilizer link bushings, "packaged" wheel bearings both front and rear and low-friction ball joints at all locations.

"We . . . have been a leader in suspension design for a long time. In terms of technical innovation, we've taken a great leap forward with this model," said Fred Schaafsma, staff engineer in charge of Corvette development and testing. He went on to say, "What we were really after was a car that handles with high input response . . . with precision and predictability . . . at all speeds." I don't think there is anyone who could disagree with him on those points.

The news in the brake department this year is the use of alloy materials. Low-drag, four-wheel power assisted disc brakes are standard and feature semi-metallic linings for outstanding fade characteristics. While the rotors continue to be vented cast-iron units (for maximum strength), the new Corvette uses aluminum instead of traditional steel on the brake rotor dust or splash shield. The brake calipers are constructed from a combination of iron and cast aluminum, which has the stiffness of steel and lightness of aluminum. Even the brake master cylinder is constructed from aluminum.

New for 1984 are the specifically designed tires from Goodyear. These provide exceptional engineering qualities including:

- ☐ Low road noise; despite blocky tread design, less road noise howl is produced without compromising road handling qualities.
- ☐ Low rolling resistance; when inflated to 35 psi, tests indicate one-half mpg fuel economy increase over base tires.
- ☐ High lateral acceleration properties which allow sidewall, tread, and carcass to maintain full tread contact under high performance driving conditions.
- ☐ Fast heat dissipation, a fundamental feature for tires when operated at high speeds over long periods of time. This helps to prevent separation of plies and compounds.
- ☐ A tread pattern offering good wet traction properties by channeling the water in order that a greater percentage of

the footprint is in contact with the road. This design is based on Goodyear's Formula One racing rain tire.

"The handling of the car is dominated by its tires as well as its structural integrity," said Dave McLellan, Corvette chief engineer.

Optional tires are from the latest in Goodyear Technology: P255/50VR16 unidirectional tires, which are mounted on special 16-inch cast aluminum wheels, each specifically designed for the left or right side of the automobile. These tires, with the VR designation, are commonly found on Europe's most exotic road cars and must be tested to meet rigid criteria for withstanding high speeds for longer durations of time compared to conventional tires.

Innovative techniques have been applied to the wheels by making the rear wheels one-half inch wider than the front. The wider rear wheels allow the rear tires to "work" harder during cornering maneuvers, resulting in more disciplined control and increased lateral capability.

The new Corvette offers an interior design that combines innovative features and advanced technology in a theme of functional elegance (Fig. 1-29).

Major new interior features include a standard electronic information system, high-performance seats, improved driver and passenger accommodations, an electronically tuned stereo radio

Fig. 1-29. Every conceivable piece of information is presented in the new Corvette Cockpit. New analog speedometer and tachometer highlight the dashboard. Other information available includes number of miles to go with present gas, instantaneous mpg, oil pressure and temperature, trip mileage, battery voltage, and coolant temperature.

with four speakers, digital clock, seek-and-scan power antenna, and side window defrosters.

A unique state-of-the-art information system is created with the sophisticated, cockpit-like instrument panel; electronic LCD speedometer and tachometer displays are flanked by digital display readouts of engine and electrical conditions. The driver information system features an on-board computer providing digital readouts of range and average mpg. Warning signals include low fuel supply, high engine oil and engine water temperatures, low oil pressure, and low voltage. The new dashboard and instrument panel are sheathed in flat black zero-gloss paint to minimize glare.

Both driver and passenger are surrounded in deep cut pile nylon carpeting covering all floor surfaces, lower door panels, rear load area sidewalls, and knee-impact areas. Newly styled standard high back bucket seats mold to the body contours while cushion and backrest lateral restraint side bolsters and manual angle adjustment combine comfort and appearance in standard full cloth trim or optional leather trim. Further interior refinements are available through an optional seat, which offers backrest lateral restraint with a power-adjusted 15-degree in-or-out bolster adjustment. A lumbar support is power-adjusted over 12 degrees of travel. The seat is trimmed in a special cloth and also includes the wool pad liner.

The Delco/Bose stereo system was designed specifically for the interior of the Corvette and offers outstanding acoustics with little or no distortion. The receiver is a Delco Electronics electronically tuned AM/FM stereo radio with auto-reverse cassette player with tone and balance controls. Four direct reflecting speakers, one in each door and one at each side of the rear compartment, reproduce the sound. Each speaker has its own equalizer and 25-watt digital mode amplifier. Dolby sound, dynamic noise reduction, and an automatic supression system complete the sound package.

Optional equipment includes dual heated sport mirrors (combined with the rear window defogger), a CB radio, and cruise control (for manual transmission.)

A full-width lift-off panel replaces the former T-top roof panel. A fiberglass roof panel with clear plastic is available as an option. The new rear hatchback design features a frameless, one-piece, tinted glass hatch, which adds to the smoother, sleeker lines of the car. The hatch is flush-hinged with the roof section forming the hinge. Luggage capacity is comparable to the 1982 model.

Power for the 1984 Corvette continues with the 205-hp 5.7 liter V-8 with Cross-Fire Fuel Injection. The engine has electronic spark control, 9.1:1 compression ratio, with 290 ft/lbs of torque at 2800 rpm. The automatic transmission is standard but the four-speed can be ordered at no charge.

A new engine accessory drive system features a serpentine double-duty belt drive that is lighter and more durable, helping to conserve engine power. A belt tensioner is employed to provide constant and uniform tension, thus helping to eliminate slippage of the multiple-grooved belt. The belt actually has six miniature V grooves on the inside of the belt drive to power the heavily-loaded accessories while the flat back side is used to drive the power steering and coolant pumps.

The electric fan is linked to coolant temperature and operates only to maintain engine temperature at or below a certain level. Normally, the cooling fan only operates when the Corvette is running under 35 mph. Air for the fuel injection system is obtained through a new split duct system that supplies cool air from the outside to the air cleaner. A single forward-mounted opening picks up the cool air and channels it along the left and right sides of the clamshell hood to the new dual inlet air cleaner. Separate vacuum-modulated doors at each intake regulate flow of the cold air to the carburetor.

A new four-speed manual transmission is available that incorporates a hydraulic clutch with a computer-controlled overdrive in the top three gears. The computer analyzes several engine functions and factors them into the overdrive system in all three overdrive gears. The four-speed automatic transmission is also computer-controlled with fourth gear providing a .70:1 overdrive.

Lightweight state-of-the-art materials continue in the engine compartment. New die-cast aluminum components include the alternator brackets, power steering elements, and air-conditioning compressor; even the engine lifting bracket is made of aluminum. For the first time in the automotive world, the propeller shaft and its yokes are made from forged aluminum.

Also new and lightweight for this year is the aluminum and plastic radiator. The core is constructed from aluminum while the side tanks are impact-resistant plastic. The SMC plastic radiator support is unique in that the plastic filler is inundated with bubbles and is approximately 27 percent lighter than standard SMC.

Chapter 2

Data, Details, and Notes

One of the questions that frequently crosses the mind of any auto enthusiast is *how much did that cost?* This question eventually leads to others, especially to those regarding the options.

The cataloging of options is not as clear cut as it first would appear. The biggest problem lies in the running changes that are made from day to day and month to month. The availability of options and even their prices change according to some unknown force in the corporate hierarchy. Just to confuse matters, promotional literature will often show and perhaps even highlight standard or optional features that were never implemented.

According to some, an additional problem has been in the making for some time now, and will undoubtedly cause problems for future restorers and enthusiasts. Apparently, it is possible to order options from GM that are not necessarily compatible, such as an exterior color and an interior color which are not listed together. This confusion is allowed under the heading of "non-recommended customer preference."

In addition to the basic data for each year and model, a complete list of options and selected notes are offered. One word of caution: Not all options were offered throughout the entire model run and it is possible that some were not offered at all. In some instances, options and standard features that normally were produced in sufficient quantities ran out and were substituted with the next year's parts.

1953

Identification

- ☐ Ignition shielding has smooth top; later units had X on top for rigidity.
- ☐ Trunk mats are numbered and have #4636966 stamped on rear of mat. Slightly smaller than the '54 and '55 trunk mats.
- ☐ Exhaust extensions extend just over one inch beyond the body. This earlier short extension did not have a cut-out section or a baffle as found on the later, longer extensions.
- ☐ Early models had a gas filler door that restricted access to a degree. A change was made between vehicles #83 and #91 that provided easier access to the gas cap.
- ☐ Two hood releases were used, one on the far left and one on the far right.
- ☐ Window bag is vinyl and is constructed of black oilcloth. It is shaped like the windows.
- ☐ Door pulls had three anchoring screws.
- ☐ Approximately the first 25 Corvettes were equipped with Chevrolet Bel Air wheelcovers.
- ☐ The valve covers look similar to the passenger car versions, however, the Corvette covers differ in having a rounded section at the top in front in order to clear the hood. The valve covers had two decals which read "BLUE FLAME" on the passenger's side and "SPECIAL" on the driver's side.
- ☐ Parking brake rod bracket is red.
- ☐ Three separate bullet-type air cleaners were used in 1953.

- ☐ A foot-operated windshield washer pump was used until approximately vehicle #175, when a vacuum system was implemented.
- ☐ The fuel filter is located just ahead of the #1 carburetor.
- ☐ Starters for 1953 are of the two field coil design.

Specifications

Base Price: $3,498.00
Chassis and Body Numbers: E53F001001 through E53F001300
I.D. Location: On plate attached to the left-front body door hinge pillar
Curb Weight: 2950 lbs.
Weight Distribution: 53/47
Turning Circle: 38 ft.
Wheelbase: 102 inches
Track, front: 57 inches, rear: 58.8 inches
Height: 52.2 inches
Length: 167.25 inches
Width: 69.8 inches
Steering Ratio: 16:1
Wheel Rim: 15 × 5K
Standard Tire Size: 6.70 × 15

Identification Numbers

Engine Prefix: 1953 engines used the prefix LAY.
Block Casting: 3701481
Head Casting: 3836066
Distributor: 1112314
Generator: 1102793
Carburetor: Carter YH-2066-S (early) and Carter YH-2066-SA (late)

Options

Factory No.	Item	Price
2934	Base Corvette	$3,498.00
101A	Heater	91.40
101B	AM radio, signal seeking	145.15

Note: Even though the heater and radio are listed as options, they were installed on each car.

Colors

Exterior Color
Polo White

Interior Color
Red

Convertible Top
Black

1954

Identification

- ☐ Exhaust extensions continued with the short design until #2524, when GM shifted to a longer 5-inch design to prevent blackening of the rear bumper. The longer design included a cut-out section that faced down, and a built-in baffle.
- ☐ Early in the '54 production run the two hood releases were merged into one hood release latch at the driver's side.
- ☐ Radios for 1954 had two white Conelrad markings.
- ☐ While early 1954 models still had the door pull retained with three anchoring screws, the later models used four screws.
- ☐ Window bags continued to be vinyl but now were red or beige and rectangular in shape.
- ☐ The first 2906 vehicles used three separate bullet-type air cleaners; later models used two pancake-type chrome air cleaners.
- ☐ The first 15 vehicles used the two-field coil starter while the remaining models used a four-field model.
- ☐ Valve cover for 1954 featured a more squared-off top in front and was retained with four mounting screws at the base of the cover.
- ☐ Decals on the modified valve cover now read "Blue Flame 150." Some covers came painted and some came chrome-plated.
- ☐ After approximately vehicle #15, the fuel filter was

switched to the right side front of the engine just in front of the fuel pump.
- ☐ Convertible tops are canvas and are tan for 1954.
- ☐ Almost all 1954s, with the exception of a few late models, were equipped with tube-type tires. The switch was made to tubeless near the end of production.
- ☐ A moisture-absorbing compound compartment was installed in the license plate cover.
- ☐ Fuel and brake lines ran on the inside of the frame members as opposed to the outside for 1953.
- ☐ Beginning with the last 600 models in 1954, folding tops came with instruction decals for operation.
- ☐ An extra fiberglass support is located behind the front fiberboard panel in the trunk.
- ☐ The engine offered in 1954 came either with 150 hp or 155 hp. The increase in horsepower came from a running change in camshaft design. The higher output cam can be identified by observing three dots between the #5 and #6 inlet cam lobe.

Specifications

Base Price: $2,774.00
Chassis and Body Numbers: E54S001001 through E54S004640

I.D. Location: On plate attached to the left-front body door hinge pillar.
Curb Weight: 2850 lbs.
Weight Distribution: 53/47
Turning Circle: 38.6 ft.
Wheelbase: 102 inches
Track, front: 57 inches, rear: 59 inches
Height: 52.2 inches
Length: 167.25 inches
Width: 69.8 inches
Steering Ratio: 16:1
Wheel Rim: 15 × 5K
Standard Tire Size: 6.70 × 15

Identification Numbers

Engine Suffix: 1954 engines used the suffix F54YG.
Block Casting: 3835911

Head Casting: 3836241
Distributor: 1112314
Generator: 1102793
Carburetor: Carter YH-2066-SA

Options

Factory No.	Item	Price
2934	Base Corvette	$2,774.00
100Q	Directional signal, Polo White	16.75
100R	Directional signal, Pennant Blue	16.75
101A	Heater	91.40
102A	AM radio, signal seeking	145.15
290B	6.70×15 whitewall tires	26.90
313M	Powerglide automatic transmission	178.35
420A	Parking brake alarm	5.65
421A	Courtesy light	4.05
422A	Windshield washer	11.85

Note: Although the Powerglide transmission is listed as an option, no cars were equipped with a manual transmission, forcing owners to purchase the optional transmission. This helped keep the base price of the car artificially low.

Colors

Exterior Color	Interior Color	Convertible Top
Polo White	Red	Beige
Black	Red	Beige
Sportsman Red	Red	Beige
Pennant Blue	Beige	Beige

1955

Identification

- ☐ Vent window locks appeared.
- ☐ Models equipped with the 265 c.i. V-8 engine had a large gold V in the word CheVrolet on the side of the front fenders.
- ☐ V-8 models were 12-volt; 6-cylinder models were 6-volt.
- ☐ Late models had the rear view mirror changed to a thumbscrew height adjuster.
- ☐ Tachometers read to 6000 rpm.
- ☐ V-8 models equipped with the optional heater had a manual heater shutoff valve located in the upper heater hose on the inner fender.
- ☐ V-8 valve covers were chrome-plated.

Specifications

Base Price: $2,774.00, 6-cyl., $2909.00, 8-cyl.
Chassis and Body Numbers: VE55S001001 through VE55S001700

I.D. Location: On plate attached to the left-front body door hinge pillar.
Curb Weight: 2850 lbs.
Weight Distribution: 53/47
Turning Circle: 39 ft.
Wheelbase: 102 inches
Track, front: 56.7 inches, rear: 58.8 inches
Height: 52.2 inches
Length: 167 inches

Width: 72.2 inches
Steering Ratio: 16.1
Wheel Rim: 15 × 5K
Standard Tire Size: 6.70 × 15

Identification Numbers

Engine Suffix: F55YG (6-cyl.), F55FG (8 cyl. with powerglide), F255GR (8-cyl., manual transmission)
Block Casting: 3835911 (6-cyl.), 3703524 (8-cyl.)
Head Casting: 3836241 (6-cyl.), 8-cyl. engines had rectangular cast mark at bottom of cylinder heads.
Distributor: 1112314 (6-cyl.), 1110855 or 1110847 (8-cyl.)
Generator: 1102793 (6-cyl.) 1102025 (8-cyl.)
Carburetor: Carter YH2066SA (6-cyl.), Carter WCFB2218S, 2351S, 2366S or 3769S (8-cyl.)

Options

Factory No.	*Item*	*Price*
100Q	Directional signal, Polo White	16.75
100R	Directional signal, Pennant Blue	16.75
101A	Heater	91.40
102A	AM radio, signal seeking	145.15
290B	6.70×15 whitewall tires	26.90
313M/N	Powerglide automatic transmission	178.35
420A	Parking brake alarm	5.65
421A	Courtesy light	4.05
422A	Windshield washer	11.85

Note: Every option listed except 101A, 102A and 290B were mandatory. The base price included a manual transmission, however, no six-cylinders have been found with a manual transmission, only the optional Powerglide. The earliest models of the production year did not have the manual transmission.

Colors

Exterior Color	*Interior Color*	*Convertible Top*
Polo White	Red	White/Beige
Harvest Gold	Yellow	Dark Green
Gypsy Red	Light Beige	Beige
Corvette Copper	Dark Beige	White
Pennant Blue	Dark Beige	Beige

1956

Identification

- ☐ Passenger seat became adjustable.
- ☐ Roll-up windows now available.
- ☐ Pushbutton door handles, locks, and latches.
- ☐ Fresh air heaters available after vehicle #150.
- ☐ Two bolt exhaust manifolds used on vehicles before #2000.
- ☐ Factory-installed oil filter appears.
- ☐ First external door handles.
- ☐ Introduction of the cast aluminum manifold. Dual four-barrel carburetors were also offered for the first time.
- ☐ Optional engines came with dual point distributors.

Specifications

Base Price: $2,900.00
Chassis and Body Numbers: E56S001001 through E56S004467

I.D. Location: On plate attached to the left-front body door hinge pillar.
Curb Weight: 3020 lbs.
Weight Distribution: 52/48
Turning Circle: 37 ft.
Wheelbase: 102 inches
Track, front: 56.7 inches, rear: 58.8 inches
Height: 52 inches

Length: 168 inches
Width: 70.5 inches
Steering Ratio: 16:1
Wheel Rim: 15 × 5K
Standard Tire Size: 6.70 × 15

Identification Numbers

Engine Suffix: FK-210 hp. (auto.), GR-225 hp. (manual), FG-225 hp. (auto.) GV-210 hp. (manual), GU-240 hp. (manual)
Block Casting: 3720991
Head Casting: Casting mark at an end of cylinder heads.
    210 hp. and early 225 hp.
    240 hp. and later 225 hp.
Distributor: 1110872, 1110879 (225 & 240 hp.)
    1110866, 1110869, 1110878 (210 hp.)
Generator: 1102020 early, 1102043 late
Carburetor: Carter WCFB2362S, 2419S

Options

Factory No.	Item	Price
101	Heater	$115.00
102	AM radio, signal seeking	185.00
107	Parking brake signal	5.00
108	Courtesy light	8.00
109	Windshield washer	11.00
290	6.70×15 whitewall tires	30.00
313	Powerglide automatic transmission	175.00
419	Auxiliary hardtop	200.00
426	Electric windows	60.00
440(series)	Color and trim combination	18.00
449	Special highlift camshaft	175.00
469	2 4-bbl. carburetors	160.00
473	Hydraulic folding top mechanism	100.00

Note: The base Corvette was delivered with a 265 c.i. engine, close ratio four-speed transmission, and manually operated soft top.

Colors

Exterior Color	Interior Color	Convertible Top	Sidewell*
Polo White	Red	White, Beige, Black	Silver
Venetian Red	Red	White, Beige, Black	Beige

Exterior Color	Interior Color	Convertible Top	Sidewell*
Aztec Copper	Beige	White, Beige	Beige
Arctic Blue	Red, Beige	White, Beige, Black	Silver
Cascade Green	Beige	White, Beige, Black	Beige
Onyx Black	Red, Beige	White, Beige, Black	Silver

*Additional Cost Item

1957

Identification

- ☐ All optional hardtops have stainless steel header trim.
- ☐ "Wonderbar" is inscribed on the AM radio.
- ☐ Many subtle differences between 1956 and 1957 models such as chrome shift knobs in 1956 and white plastic in 1975.

Specifications

Base Price: $3,176.32
Chassis and Body Numbers: E57S1001 through E57S106339

I.D. Location: On plate attached to the left-front body door hinge pillar.
Curb Weight: 2985 lbs.
Weight Distribution: 52/48
Turning Circle: 39 ft.
Wheelbase: 102
Track, front: 57 inches, rear: 59 inches
Height: 52
Length: 168
Width: 70.5
Steering Ratio: 16:1
Wheel Rim: 15 × 5K
Standard Tire Size: 6.70 × 15

Identification Numbers

Engine Suffix: EF-220 hp. (manual), FH-220 hp. (auto.), EH-245 hp. (manual) FG-270 hp. (auto.), EM-250 hp. (manual), FK-250 hp. (auto.), EG-270 hp. (manual), EL-283 hp. (manual), EN-283 hp. (manual with air intake)

Block Casting: 3731548

Head Casting: All except 283 hp. ▬
              All 283 hp. ⊥

Distributor: 1110891 (220, 245, 270 hp.) 1110906 (250 hp., auto.), 1110889, 1110905 (250, 283 hp., manual), 1110908 (manual, special high performance)

Generator: 1102043 (standard tachometer drive)

Carburetor: Carter WCFB2366SA, 2655S (220 hp.), 2626S, 2627S, 2613S, 2614S (245, 270 hp.)

Options

Factory No.		*Price*
101	Heater	$110.00
102	AM radio, signal seeking	185.00
107	Parking brake alarm	5.00
108	Courtesy light	8.00
109	Windshield washer	11.00
276	Five 15×5.5-inch wheels	N/C
290	6.70×15 whitewall tires	30.00
313	Powerglide automatic transmission	175.00
419	Auxiliary hardtop	200.00
426	Power windows	55.00
440(series)	Color and trim combination	18.00
469A	2-4 bbl. carburetors, 245 hp.	140.00
469B	2-4 bbl. carburetors, 270 hp.	170.00
473	Hydraulic power top	130.00
579A	Fuel injection, 250 hp.	450.00
579B	Fuel injection, 283 hp.	450.00
579E	Fuel Injection, 283 hp.	675.00
677	Positraction, 3.70:1 axle	45.00
678	Positraction, 4.11:1 axle	45.00
679	Positraction, 4.56:1 axle	45.00
684	Heavy duty racing suspension	725.00
685	4-speed transmission	175.00

Note: This is the first year for the four-speed transmission. It was not available, though, until sometime after May 1, 1957.

Colors

Exterior Color	Interior Color	Convertible Top	Sidewell*
Polo White	Red, Beige	White, Beige, Black	Silver
Venetian Red	Red, Beige	White, Beige, Black	Beige
Aztec Copper	Beige	White, Beige	Beige
Arctic Blue	Red, Beige	White, Beige, Black	Silver
Cascade Green	Beige	White, Beige, Black	Beige
Onyx Black	Red, Beige	White, Beige, Black	Silver
Inca Silver	Red, Beige	White, Black	Imperial, Ivory

*Additional Cost Item

1958

Identification

- ☐ For this year only, dots replace lines representing speed on the speedometer.
- ☐ All paint now is acrylic lacquer. Previously, the paint was nitrocellulose lacquer. Only exception: Inca Silver.
- ☐ The hood brace was switched from the right side to the left side during a running change at some point in the year.
- ☐ Introduction of the 9-tooth grill as opposed to the older 13-tooth type.
- ☐ Generator also switched from left side to the right side.
- ☐ Seat belts became standard.
- ☐ Early vehicles did not have the rear fender reflector.

Specifications

Base Price: $3,591.00
Chassis and Body Numbers: J58S100001 through J58S109168

I.D. Location: On plate attached to the left-front body door hinge pillar.
Curb Weight: 3050 lbs.
Weight Distribution: 53/47
Turning Circle: 39 ft.
Wheelbase: 102 inches
Track, front: 57 inches, rear: 59 inches

Height: 52 inches
Length: 177.2 inches
Width: 72.8 inches
Steering Ratio: 21:1 std., 16:3 optional
Wheel Rim: 15 × 5K
Standard Tire Size: 6.70 × 15

Identification Numbers

Engine Suffix: CQ-230 hp. (manual), CT-245 hp. (manual), CU-270 hp. (manual), DJ-245 hp. (auto.), DG-230 hp. (auto.), CS-290 hp. (manual), CR-250 hp. (manual), DH-250 hp. (auto.)
Block Casting: 3737739, 3756519
Head Casting: All except 290 hp.
All 290 hp.
Distributor: 1110890 (230 hp.), 1110891 (245, 270 hp.), 1110915 (250, 275 hp.), 1110914 (290 hp., tachometer drive)
Generator: 1102043 (standard tachometer drive), 1102059 (290 hp. non-tachometer drive)
Carburetor: Carter WCFB2668S, 2669S, 3059S (230 hp.), 2626S, 3181S, 2627S, 2362S (245 hp.), 2613S, 3182S, 2614S (270 hp.)

Options

Factory No.	*Item*	*Price*
101	Heater	96.85
102	AM radio, signal seeking	144.45
107	Parking brake alarm	5.40
108	Courtesy light	6.50
109	Windshield washer	16.15
276	Five 15×5.5-inch wheels	N/C
290	6.70×15 whitewall tires	31.55
313	Powerglide automatic transmission	188.30
419	Auxiliary hardtop	215.20
426	Electric power windows	59.20
440(series)	Color and trim combination	16.15
469	2-4 bbl. carburetors, 245 hp.	150.65
469C	2-4 bbl. carburetors, 270 hp.	182.95
473	Hydraulic power top	139.90
579	Fuel injection, 250 hp.	484.20
579D	Fuel injection, 290 hp.	484.20
677	Positraction, 3.70:1 axle	48.45

Factory No.	Item	Price
678	Positraction, 4.11:1 axle	48.45
679	Positraction, 4.56:1 axle	48.45
684	Heavy duty brakes and suspension	780.10
685	4-speed transmission	215.20

Note: Option 313, Powerglide automatic transmission, was not available with options 469 or 579.

Colors

Exterior Color	Interior Color	Convertible Top	Sidewell*
Snowcrest White	Charcoal, Red, Blue/Gray	Black, White, Blue-Gray	Inca Silver
Signet Red	Charcoal Red	Black, White	Snowcrest White
Panama Yellow	Charcoal	Black, White	Snowcrest White
Regal Turquoise	Charcoal	Black, White	Snowcrest White
Silver Blue	Charcoal, Blue/Gray	White, Blue/Gray	
Charcoal	Charcoal, Blue/Gray, Red	Black, White	

*Additional Cost Item
 May also be body color

1959

Identification

- ☐ Reverse lockout appears on the shifter.
- ☐ Tachometers read to 7000 rpm.
- ☐ Slotted hubcaps appear.
- ☐ Package tray is added to the underside of the passenger grab bar.
- ☐ Very late in the production run the valve cover bolt pattern changes from staggered holes to straight across.

Specifications

Base Price: $3,875.00
Chassis and Body Numbers: J59S100001 through J59S109670

I.D. Location: On plate attached to the left-front body door hinge plate.
Curb Weight: 3080 lbs.
Weight Distribution: 53/47
Turning Circle: 39 ft.
Wheelbase: 102 inches
Track, front: 57 inches, rear: 59 inches
Height: 52.4 inches
Length: 177.2 inches
Width: 72.8 inches
Steering Ratio: 21:1 std., 16.3:1 optional

Wheel Rim: 15 × 5K
Standard Tire Size: 6.70 × 15

Identification Numbers

Engine Suffix: CQ-230 hp. (manual), CT-245 hp. (manual), CU-270 hp. (manual), CS-290 hp. (manual), CR-250 hp. (manual), DH-250 hp. (auto.), DJ-245 hp. (auto.), DG-230 hp. (auto.)
Block Casting: 3737739, 3756519
Head Casting: All except 290 hp.
All 290 hp.
Distributor: 1110946 (230 hp.), 1110891 (245, 270 hp.), 1110915 (250 hp.), 1110914 (290 hp., tachometer drive)
Generator: 1101043 (standard tachometer drive), 1102059, 1102173 (290 hp. non-tachometer drive)
Carburetor: Carter WCFB2669S, 3059S, 2818S (230 hp.), 2626S, 3181S, 2627S, 2362S (245 hp.), 2613S, 3182S, 2614S (270 hp.)

Options

Factory No.	*Item*	*Price*
101	Heater	$102.25
102	AM radio, signal seeking	149.80
107	Parking brake alarm	5.40
108	Courtesy light	6.50
109	Windshield washer	16.15
261	Sunshades	10.80
276	Five 15×5.5-inch wheels	N/C
290	6.70×15 whitewall tires	31.55
313	Powerglide automatic transmission	199.10
419	Auxiliary hardtop	236.75
426	Electric power windows	59.20
469	2-4 bbl. carburetors, 245 hp.	150.65
469C	2-4 bbl. carburetors, 270 hp.	182.95
473	Hydraulic power top	139.90
579	Fuel injection, 250 hp.	484.20
579D	Fuel injection, 290 hp.	484.20
675	Positraction	48.45
684	Heavy duty brakes and suspension	425.05
685	4-speed transmission	188.30
686	Metallic brakes	26.90
1625	Gasoline tank, 24 gallon	161.40

Colors

Exterior Color	Interior Color	Convertible Top	Sidewell*
Snowcrest White	Black, Blue, Turquoise, Red	Turquoise, Light Blue, Black, White	Inca Silver
Classic Cream	Black	Black, White	Snowcrest White
Roman Red	Black, Red	Black, White	Snowcrest White
Crown Sapphire	Turquoise	White, Turquoise	Snowcrest White
Frost Blue	Blue, Red	White, Light Blue	Snowcrest White
Inca Silver	Black, Red	Black, White	Snowcrest White
Tuxedo Black	Black, Blue, Red	Black, White	Inca Silver

*Additional Cost Item
May also be body color

1960

Identification

- ☐ Aluminum heads were offered but were withdrawn quickly due to poor quality.
- ☐ New-style aluminum radiator offered with fuel-injected engine.
- ☐ After approximately 3000 vehicles were constructed, the vehicle identification number (VIN) was moved from the left-front body door hinge pillar to the steering column under the hood.
- ☐ Red and blue bar added over the word "Corvette" behind the passenger assist bar.

Specifications

Base Price: $3,872.00
Chassis and Body Numbers: 00867S100001 through 00876S110261

I.D. Location: On plate attached to the steering column under the hood.
Curb Weight: 3104 lbs.
Weight Distribution: 53/47
Turning Circle: 39 ft.
Wheelbase: 102 inches
Track, front: 57 inches, rear: 59 inches
Height: 52.3 inches
Length: 177.2 inches

Width: 72.8 inches
Steering Ratio: 21:1 std., 16.3:1 optional
Wheel Rim: 15 × 5K
Standard Tire Size: 6.70 × 15

Identification Numbers

Engine Suffix: DJ-245 hp. (auto.), DG-230 hp. (auto.), CQ-230 hp. (manual), CT-245 hp. (manual), CU-270 hp. (manual), CR-275 hp. (manual) CY-275 hp. (manual w/ alum. heads), CS-315 hp. (manual), CZ-315 hp. (manual w/ alum. heads)
Block Casting: 3737730, 3756519
Head Casting: All except 315 hp. ▲
 All 315 hp. ⌴
Distributor: 1110946 (230 hp.), 1110891 (245, 270 hp.), 1110915 (275 hp.), 1110914 (315 hp., tachometer drive)
Generator: 1102043 (standard tachometer drive), 1102173 (315 hp., non-tachometer drive)
Carburetor: Carter WCFB2669S, 3059S, 2818S (230 hp.), 2626S, 3181S, 2419S, 2627S 2362S (245 hp.), 2613S, 3182S, 2614S (270 hp.)

Options

Factory No.	Item	Price
101	Heater	$102.25
102	AM radio, signal seeking	137.75
107	Parking brake alarm	5.40
108	Courtesy light	6.50
109	Windshield washer	16.50
121	Fan drive, temperature controlled	21.55
261	Sunshades	10.80
276	Five 15×5.5-inch wheels	N/C
290	6.70×15 whitewall tires	31.55
313	Powerglide automatic transmission	199.10
419	Auxiliary hardtop	236.75
426	Electric power windows	59.20
469	2-4 bbl. carburetors, 245 hp.	150.65
469	2-4 bbl. carburetors, 270 hp.	182.95
473	Hydraulic power top	139.90
579	Fuel injection, 275 hp.	484.20
579	Fuel injection, 315 hp.	484.20
675	Positraction	43.05

Factory No.	Item	Price
685	4-speed transmission	188.30
686	Metallic brakes	26.90
687	Heavy duty brakes and special steering	333.60
1625	Gasoline tank, 24 gallon	161.40

Colors

Exterior Color	Interior Color	Convertible Top	Sidewell*
Ermine White	Black, Blue, Red, Turquoise	Light Blue, Black, White	Sateen Silver
Roman Red	Black, Red	Black, White	Ermine White
Honduras Maroon	Black	Black	Ermine White
Horizon Blue	Black, Blue, Red	Light Blue, Black, White	Ermine White
Tasco Turquoise	Black, Turquoise	Light Blue, Black, White	Ermine White
Cascade Green	Black	Light Blue, Black, White	Ermine White
Sateen Silver	Black, Blue, Red, Turquoise	Light Blue, Black, White	Ermine White
Tuxedo Black	Black, Blue, Red, Turquoise	Light Blue, Black, White	Sateen Silver

* Additional Cost Item
  May also be body color

1961

Identification

- ☐ Gas filler door now has side hinges instead of top hinges.
- ☐ Aluminum radiator becomes standard.
- ☐ Headlight bezels are painted body color vs. chrome.
- ☐ Windshield washer reservoir is on the left side for carbureted engines and on the right side for fuel-injected engines.

Specifications

Base Price: $3,943.00
Chassis and Body Numbers: 10867S100001 through 10867S110939

I.D. Location: On plate attached to the steering column under the hood.
Curb Weight: 3108 lbs.
Weight Distribution: 53/47
Turning Circle: 39 ft.
Wheelbase: 102 inches
Track, front: 57 inches, rear: 59 inches
Height: 52.9 inches
Length: 176.7 inches
Width: 70.4 inches
Steering Ratio: 21:1 std., 16.3:1 optional
Wheel Rim: 15 × 5K
Standard Tire Size: 6.70 × 15

Identification Numbers

Engine Suffix: CQ-230 hp. (manual), CT-245 hp. (manual), CU-270 hp. (manual), CR-275 hp. (manual), CS-315 hp. (manual), DJ-245 hp. (auto.), DG-230 hp. (auto.)
Block Casting: 2756519
Head Casting: All except 275, 315 hp. ▲
All 275 and 315 hp. ▬
Distributor: 1111500, 1110946 (230 hp.), 1110891 (245, 275 hp.), 1110915 (275 hp.), 1110914 (315 hp., tachometer drive)
Generator: 1102043 (standard tachometer drive), 1102173, 1102268 (315 hp., non-tachometer drive)
Carburetor: Carter WCFB2669S, 3059S, 2818S (230 hp.), 2626S, 3181S, 2419S, 2627S, 2362S (245 hp.), 2613S, 3182S, 2614S (270 hp.)

Options

Factory No.	Item	Price
101	Heater	$102.25
102	AM radio, signal seeking	137.75
276	Five 15×5.5-inch wheels	N/C
290	6.70×15 whitewall tires	31.55
313	Powerglide automatic transmission	199.10
419	Auxiliary hardtop	236.75
426	Electric power windows	59.20
441	Direct flow exhaust	N/C
469	2-4 bbl. carburetors, 245 hp.	150.65
468	2-4 bbl. carburetors, 270 hp.	182.95
353	Fuel injection, 275 hp.	484.20
354	Fuel injection, 315 hp.	484.20
473	Hydraulic power top	161.40
675	Positraction	43.05
685	4-speed transmission	188.30
686	Metallic brakes	37.70
687	Heavy duty brakes and special steering	333.60
1625A	Gasoline tank, 24 gallon	161.40

Note: Additional standard equipment included windshield washers, courtesy lights, sunshades, parking brake warning light and a temperature controlled radiator fan. Option 313, Powerglide automatic transmission, was not available with options 353, 354 or 468.

Colors

Exterior Color	Interior Color	Convertible Top	Sidewell*
Ermine White	Black, Red, Blue, Fawn	Black, White	Sateen Silver
Roman Red	Black, Red	Black, White	Ermine White
Jewel Blue	Black, Blue	Black, White	Ermine White
Honduras Maroon	Black, Fawn	Black, White	Ermine White
Fawn Beige	Black, Red, Fawn	Black, White	Ermine White
Sateen Silver	Black, Red, Fawn	Black, White	Ermine White
Tuxedo Black	Black, Red, Blue, Fawn	Black, White	Sateen Silver

* Additional Cost Item
  May also be body color

1962

Identification

- ☐ Introduction of the 327 c.i. engine.
- ☐ All distributors have tachometer drive feature.
- ☐ Temperature gauge changes from 220° to 240° limit late in the production run.
- ☐ Grille is black.
- ☐ Offset cove color option is no longer available.
- ☐ Early vehicles had no paint between rocker panel ribs; later vehicles had black paint between rocker panel ribs.

Specifications

Base Price: $4,038.00
Chassis and Body Numbers: 20867S1000001 through
20867S114531

I.D. Location: On plate attached to the steering column under the hood.
Curb Weight: 3137 lbs.
Weight Distribution: 53/47
Turning Circle: 39 ft.
Wheelbase: 102 inches
Track, front: 57 inches, rear: 59 inches
Height: 52.9 inches
Length: 176.7 inches
Width: 70.4 inches
Steering Ratio: 21:1 std., 16.3:1 optional
Wheel Rim: 15 × 5K
Standard Tire Size: 6.70 × 15

Identification Numbers

Engine Suffix: RC-250 hp. (manual), RF-360 hp., (manual), RD-300 hp. (manual), SC-250 hp. (auto.) RE-340 hp. (manual), SD-300 hp. (auto.)
Block Casting: 3782870
Head Casting: All except 250 hp. ▲
All 250 hp. ▄
Distributor: 1110984, (250, 300 hp.), 1110985 (340 hp.), 1110990, 1111011 (360 hp.)
Generator: 1102268 (360 hp. and others, early)
1102174 (all others except early)
Carburetor: Carter WCFB3191S, (250 hp.), 3269S (300, 340 hp.)

Options

Factory No.	*Item*	*Price*
102	AM Radio, signal seeking	$137.75
242	Crankcase vent	5.40
276	Five 15×5.5-inch wheels	N/C
313	Powerglide automatic transmission	199.10
419	Auxiliary hardtop	236.75
426	Electric power windows	59.20
441	Direct flow exhaust	N/C
473	Hydraulic power top	161.40

Factory No.	Item	Price
488	Gasoline tank, 24 gallon	118.40
582	Fuel injection, 360 hp.	484.20
583	327 c.i. engine, 300 hp.	53.80
396	327 c.i. engine, 340 hp.	107.60
675	Positraction rear axle	43.05
685	4-speed transmission	188.30
686	Metallic brakes	37.70
687	Heavy duty brakes and special steering	333.60
1832	6.70×15 whitewall tires	31.55

Note: Except for those Corvettes exported, the heater became standard equipment. Option 313, Powerglide automatic transmission, was not available with options 396 or 582.

Colors

Exterior Color	Interior Color	Convertible Top
Ermine White	Black, Red, Fawn	Black, White
Almond Beige	Red, Fawn	Black, White
Fawn Beige	Red, Fawn	Black, White
Roman Red	Black, Red, Fawn	Black, White
Honduras Maroon	Black, Fawn	Black, White
Sateen Silver	Black, Red	Black, White
Tuxedo Black	Black, Red, Fawn	Black, White

1963

Identification

- ☐ First year of the Sting Ray.
- ☐ Faceplate over the glove box door is covered with plastic.
- ☐ Early vehicles have a storage compartment underneath the seats; discontinued sometime mid-year.
- ☐ Split-window design particular to this year only.
- ☐ Cast aluminum knock-off wheels were available in either two-bar or three-bar design. The two-bar design was dropped during a running change.

- ☐ Steering wheel is color-coded to the interior and is not wood.
- ☐ Shifter knobs were black plastic.
- ☐ Radio in early vehicles is AM Wonderbar; changed to AM/FM later.
- ☐ Door latch release knob is plastic.

Specifications

Base Price: $4,257.00 Sport Coupe, $4,047.00 Convertible
Chassis and Body Numbers: 30867S100001 through 30867S121513 (30867-Convertible, 30837-Coupes)

I.D. Location: High pillar cross brace under glove box.
Curb Weight: 3150 lbs.
Weight Distribution: 48/52
Turning Circle: 41.9 ft.
Wheelbase: 98 inches
Track, front: 56.3 inches, rear: 57 inches
Height: 49.8 inches
Length: 175.3 inches
Width: 69.6 inches
Steering Ratio: 20.2:1 std., 17.6:1 optional and w/power steering
Wheel Rim: 15 × 5K
Standard Tire Size: 6.70 × 15

Identification Numbers

Engine Suffix: RC-250 hp. (manual), RD-300 (manual), RE-340 hp. (manual), RF-360 hp., (manual), SC-250 hp. (auto.), SD-300 hp. (auto.)
Block Casting: 3782870
Head Casting: All except 250 hp. ▲
            All 250 hp. ▬
Distributor: 1111024 (250, 300, 340 hp.), 1111022 (360 hp.)
Carburetor: Carter WCFB3501S, 3500S, (250 hp.), 3460S, 3461S, (300, 360 hp.)

Options

Factory No.	Item	Price
A01	Soft ray tinted glass, all windows	$16.15
A02	Soft ray tinted glass, windshield	10.80
A31	Electric power windows	59.20

Factory No.	Item	Price
C07	Auxiliary hardtop	236.75
C48	Heater and defroster deletion for credit	100.00
C60	Air conditioning	421.80
G81	Positraction	43.05
G91	Special highway axle, 3.08:1	2.20
J50	Power brakes	43.05
J65	Sintered metallic power brakes	37.70
L75	327 c.i. engine, 300 hp.	53.80
L76	327 c.i. engine, 340 hp.	107.60
L84	327 c.i. engine, 360 hp., Fuel Injection	430.40
M20	4-speed transmission	188.30
M35	Powerglide automatic transmission	199.10
N03	Gasoline tank, 36 gallon (coupe only)	202.30
N11	Off-road exhaust	37.70
N34	Woodgrained plastic steering wheel	16.15
N40	Power steering	75.35
P48	Cast aluminum knock-off wheels	322.80
P91	6.70×15 blackwall nylon tires	15.70
P92	6.70×15 whitewall nylon tires	31.55
T86	Back-up lights	10.80
U65	AM radio, signal seeking (early models)	137.75
U69	AM/FM radio	174.35
Z06	Special performance equipment (early coupe)	1818.45

Note: Z06 was not available on roadsters until late in the year. At year's end the option was reduced to $1293.95 and excluded the knock-off wheels and the 36-gallon gasoline tank.

Colors

Factory Number	Exterior Color	Interior Color	Convertible Top
936	Ermine White	Black, Red, Dark Blue, Saddle	Black, White, Beige
932	Saddle Tan	Black, Red, Saddle	Black, White, Beige
923	Riverside Red	Black, Red, Saddle	Black, White, Beige
912	Silver Blue	Black, Dark Blue	Black, White, Beige

Factory Number	Exterior Color	Interior Color	Convertible Top
916	Daytona Blue	Red, Saddle, Dark Blue	Black, White, Beige
941	Sebring Silver	Black, Red, Dark Blue, Saddle	Black, White, Beige
900	Tuxedo Black	Black, Red, Saddle	Black, White, Beige

1964

Identification

- ☐ Console trim panel unit is now one piece.
- ☐ Changes of the type above exemplify the many minor changes that were made between the 1963 and 1964 model years. Some have calculated that over 1,000 changes were made. The more noticeable changes include full rear window replacing the split window, different rocker panels and hubcaps, deletion of the hood grilles and door pillar lace.

Specifications

Base Price: $4,252.00 Coupe, $4,037.00 Convertible Chassis and Body Numbers: 40867S100001 through
          40867S122229
          (40837-Coupe)

I.D. Location: Hinge pillar cross brace under glove box.
Curb Weight: 3180 lbs.
Weight Distribution: 48/52
Turning Circle: 41.9 ft.
Wheelbase: 98 inches
Track, front: 56.3 inches, rear: 57 inches
Height: 49.8 inches
Length: 175.3 inches
Width: 69.6 inches
Steering Ratio: 20.2:1 std., 17.6:1 optional and w/power steering

Wheel Rim: 15 × 55K
Standard Tire Size: 6.70 × 15

Identification Numbers

Engine Suffix: RX-375 hp. (manual/trans. ign.) RU-365 hp. (manual/trans. ign./AC), RT-365 hp. (manual/trans. ign.), RR-365 hp. (manual/AC), RE-365 hp. (manual), RD-300 hp. (manual), RQ-300 hp. (manual/AC), SD-300 hp. (auto.), SL-300 hp. (auto/AC), SK-250 hp. (auto.A/C), SC-250 hp. (auto.) RP-250 hp. (manual/AC), RC-250 hp. (manual)

Block Casting: 3782870

Head Casting: All except 250 hp. ▲
All 250 hp.

Distributor: 1111024 (250, 300 hp.), 1111062 (365 hp.), 1111060 (365 hp./trans, ign.), 1111063 (375 hp.), 1111064 (375 hp./trans. ign.).

Carburetor: Carter WCFB3501S, 3500S (250 hp.), Carter AFB3720S, 3721S (300 hp.) Holley R2818A (365 hp.)

Options

Factory No.	*Item*	*Price*
A01	Soft ray tinted glass, all windows	$16.15
A02	Soft ray tinted glass, windshield	10.80
A31	Electric windows	59.20
C07	Auxiliary hardtop	236.75
C48	Heater and defroster deletion for credit	100.00
C60	Air conditioning	421.80
F40	Front and rear suspension, special	37.70
G81	Positraction	43.05
G91	Special highway axle, 3.08:1	2.20
J50	Power brakes	43.05
J56	Sintered metallic brake package	629.50
J65	Sintered metallic power brakes	53.80
K66	Transistorized ignition system	75.35
L75	327 c.i. engine, 300 hp.	53.80
L76	327 c.i. engine, 365 hp.	107.60
L84	327 c.i. engine, 375 hp.	538.00
M20	4-speed transmission	188.30
M35	Powerglide automatic transmission	199.10
N03	Gasoline tank, 36 gallon (coupe only)	202.30

Factory No.	Item	Price
N11	Off-road exhaust	37.70
N40	Power steering	75.35
P48	Cast aluminum knock-off wheels	322.80
P91	6.70×15 blackwall nylon tires	15.70
P92	6.70×15 whitewall nylon tires	31.85
T86	Back-up lights	10.80
U69	AM/FM radio	176.50

Note: Option M35, Powerglide automatic transmission, was not available with options L76 or L84.

Option N11, off-road exhaust, was not available with the 250 hp. engine or option M35.

Option C60, air conditioning, was not available with option L84.

Option K66, transistorized ignition, was not available with option L75.

Options J56 and F40, sintered metallic brakes and special front and rear suspension, were only available with option L84 in conjunction with M20 and positraction.

Colors

Factory Number	Exterior Color	Interior Color	Convertible Top
936	Ermine White	Black, Red, Saddle, Silver, White, Dark Blue	Black, White, Beige
932	Saddle Tan	Saddle, White	Black, White, Beige
923	Riverside Red	Black, Red, Silver, White	Black, White, Beige
912	Silver Blue	Black, White, Dark Blue	Black, White, Beige
916	Daytona Blue	Silver, White, Dark Blue	Black, White, Beige
940	Satin Silver	Black, Red, Silver, White, Dark Blue	Black, White, Beige
900	Tuxedo Black	Black, Red, Silver, White	Black, White, Beige

1965

Identification

- ☐ Introduction of the power antenna as standard equipment.
- ☐ Introduction of disc brakes.
- ☐ Louvers on the side of the front fenders were opened up and became functional.
- ☐ Rear carpeting is changed from separate pieces to molded design.
- ☐ Powerglide shift pattern changes from staggered to straight.

Specifications

Base Price: $4,321.00 Coupe, $4,106.00 Convertible
Chassis and Body Numbers: 19467S100001 through 19467S123562 (194375-Coupe)

I.D. Location: Hinge pillar cross brace under glove box.
Curb Weight: 3230 lbs.
Weight Distribution: 50/50
Turning Circle: 41.6 ft.
Wheelbase: 98 inches
Track, front: 56.8 inches, rear: 57.6 inches
Height: 49.8 inches
Length: 175.1 inches
Width: 69.6 inches

Steering Ratio: 20.2:1 std., 17.6:1 optional and w/power steering.
Wheel Rim: 15 × 5.5K
Standard Tire Size: 7.75 × 15

Identification Numbers

Engine Suffix: IF-425 hp. (396 c.i., manual), HN-375 hp. (manual/trans. ign.), HM-365 hp. (manual/trans. ign./AC), HL-365 hp. (manual/trans ign.), HK-365 hp. (manual/AC), HH-365 hp. (manual), HW-350 hp. (manual/trans. ign./AC), HV-350 hp. (manual/trans. ign.), HU-350 hp. (manual/AC), HT-350 hp. (manual), HG-375 hp. (manual), HF-300 hp. (manual), HJ-300 hp. (manual/AC), HP-300 hp. (auto.), HR-300 hp. (auto./AC), HQ-250 hp. (auto./AC), HO-250 hp. (auto.) HI-250 hp. (manual/AC), HE-250 hp. (manual)

Block Casting: 3782870 ▄▟

Head Casting: All 327 c.i. engines.

Distributor: 1111076 (250, 300 hp.), 1111070 (375 hp.), 1111087 (350 hp.), 1111064 (375 hp./trans. ign.), 1111157 (350 hp./trans. ign.), 1111093 (425 hp.), 1111024 (365 hp.)

Carburetor: Carter WCFB3696S, 3687S (250 hp.), AFB3720SA, 3721SA (300 hp.), Holley R2818A (350, 365 hp.), R3124A (425 hp.)

Options

Factory No.	Item	Price
A01	Soft ray tinted glass, all windows	$16.15
A02	Soft ray tinted glass, windshield	10.80
A31	Electric power windows	59.20
C07	Auxiliary hardtop	236.75
C48	Heater and defroster deletion for credit	100.00
C60	Air conditioning	421.80
F40	Front and rear suspension, special	37.70
G81	Positraction	43.05
G91	Special highway axle, 3.08:1	2.20
J50	Power brakes	43.05
J61	Drum brake substitution for credit	64.50
K66	Transistorized ignition system	75.35
L75	327 c.i. engine, 300 hp.	53.80
L76	327 c.i. engine, 365 hp.	129.15
L78	396 c.i. engine, 425 hp.	292.70

Factory No.	Item	Price
L79	327 c.i. engine, 350 hp.	107.60
L84	327 c.i. engine, 375 hp., Fuel Injection	538.00
M20	4-speed transmission	188.30
M22	4-speed close ratio H.D. transmission	236.95
M35	Powerglide automatic transmission	199.10
N03	Gasoline tank, 36 gallon (coupe only)	202.30
N11	Off-road exhaust	36.90
N14	Side mount exhaust system	134.50
N32	Teakwood steering wheel	48.45
N36	Telescoping steering column	43.05
N40	Power steering	96.85
P48	Cast aluminum knock-off wheels	322.80
P92	7.75×15 whitewall Rayon tires	31.85
T01	7.75×15 goldwall Nylon tires	50.05
U69	AM/FM radio	203.40
Z01	Backup lights and interior day/night mirror	16.16

Note: Option F40, special front and rear suspension, was available only with options L84 or L78 in conjunction with option M20 and positraction.

Colors

Factory Number	Exterior Color	Interior Color	Convertible Top
CC	Ermine White	Black, Red, Saddle, Silver, Blue, White, Green, Maroon	Black, White, Beige
XX	Goldwood Yellow	Black, White	Black, White, Beige
UU	Rally Red	Black, Red, White	Black, White, Beige
MM	Milano Maroon	Black, Saddle, White, Maroon	Black, White, Beige
FF	Nassau Blue	Black, Blue, White	Black, White, Beige
GG	Glen Green	Black, Saddle, White, Green	Black, White, Beige
QQ	Silver Pearl	Black, Red, Silver	Black, White, Beige
AA	Tuxedo Black	Black, Red, Saddle, Silver, Blue, White, Green, Maroon	Black, White, Beige

1966

Identification

- ☐ On the coupe, the air vents are removed from the B pillar area just forward of the rear window.
- ☐ Exhaust bezels change from stainless steel to chrome plating.
- ☐ Headliners change from fiberboard to vinyl.
- ☐ Door handle pulls are now chrome.
- ☐ First year for the headrest option.
- ☐ Introduction of the 427 c.i. engine.
- ☐ Cast aluminum wheels have brush-finished center section

instead of chrome-plated section as on wheels offered previously.

Specifications

Base Price: $4,295.00 Coupe, $4,084.00 Convertible
Chassis and Body Numbers: 194676S100001 through
                                194676S127720 (194367-Coupe)

I.D. Location: Hinge pillar cross brace under glove box.
Curb Weight: 3360 lbs.
Weight Distribution: 51.5/48.5
Turning Circle: 41.6 ft.
Wheelbase: 98 inches
Track, front: 56.8 inches, rear: 57.6 inches
Height: 49.8 inches
Length: 175.1 inches
Width: 69.6 inches
Steering Ratio: 20.2:1 std., 17.6:1 optional and w/power steering.
Wheel Rim: 15 × 5.5K
Standard Tire Size: 7.75 × 15

Identification Numbers

Engine Suffix: 327 c.i. : HE (manual), HH (A.I.R./California), HR (A.I.R./California/auto.), HD (S.H.P./A.I.R./California), HO (auto), HT (S.H.P.), HP (power steering), KH (S.H.P./A.I.R./California/AC)
          427 c.i.: IK (S.H.P./hydraulic lifter), IL (HP), IM (A.I.R./California), IP (S.H.P.), IQ (auto.), IR (A.I.R./California/auto.)
Note: HP—high performance, S.H.P.—special high performance, A.I.R.—air injection reactor
Block Casting: 3858174, most 327 c.i. engines, until late in production when 3892657 was used. 3869942, all 427 c.i. engines.
Head Casting: All 327 c.i. engines. ▄▄

Distributor: 1111117, (300 hp.), 1111141, 1111142 (390 hp.), 1111156 (350 hp.), 1111093, (425 hp.)
Carburetor: Holley R3367A, B34166A (300, 350 hp., 327 c.i. engines), R3370A, R3433A (390 hp.), R3247A (425 hp., 427 c.i.)

77

Options

Factory No.	Item	Price
A01	Soft ray tinted glass, all windows	$15.80
A02	Soft ray tinted glass, windshield	10.55
A31	Electric power windows	59.20
A82	Headrests	42.15
A85	Shoulder harness	26.35
C07	Auxiliary hardtop	231.75
C48	Heater and defroster deletion for credit	97.85
C60	Air conditioning	412.90
F41	Front and rear suspension, special	36.90
G81	Positraction	42.15
J50	Power brakes	43.05
J56	Heavy duty brakes, special	342.30
K19	Air injection reactor	NC
K66	Transistorized ignition system	73.75
L36	427 c.i. engine, 390 hp.	181.20
L72	427 c.i. engine, 425 hp.	312.85
L79	327 c.i. engine, 350 hp.	105.35
M20	4-speed transmission	184.30
M21	4-speed close ratio transmission	184.30
M22	4-speed close ratio transmission, heavy duty	237.00
M35	Powerglide automatic transmission	194.35
N03	Gasoline tank, 36 gallon	198.05
N11	Off-road exhaust	36.90
N14	Side mount exhaust system	131.65
N32	Teakwood steering wheel	48.45
N36	Telescopic steering wheel	42.15
N40	Power steering	94.80
N48	Cast aluminum bolt-on wheels	326.00
P92	7.75×15 whitewall Rayon tires	31.30
T01	7.75×15 goldwall Nylon tires	46.55
U69	AM/FM radio	199.10
V74	Traffic hazard lamp switch	11.60

Colors

Factory Number	Exterior Color	Interior Color	Convertible Top
972	Ermine White	Black, Red, Saddle, Silver, Bright Blue, White-Blue, Green, Blue	Black, White, Beige
984	Sunfire Yellow	Black	Black, White, Beige
974	Rally Red	Black, Red	Black, White, Beige
988	Milano Maroon	Black, Saddle	Black, White, Beige
980	Trophy Blue	Black, Blue, Bright Blue	Black, White, Beige
978	Laguna Blue	Black, Blue, Bright Blue	Black, White, Beige
976	Nassau Blue	Black, Blue, Bright Blue, White-Blue	Black, White, Beige
982	Mosport Green	Black, Green	Black, White, Beige
986	Silver Pearl	Black, Silver	Black, White, Beige
900	Tuxedo Black	Black, Red, Saddle, Silver, Bright Blue, White-Blue, Green, Blue	Black, White, Beige

1967

Identification

- ☐ Bolt-on cast aluminum wheels replace the knockoff wheel due to increased pressure by the federal government for a safer wheel.
- ☐ Standard wheel size increases to six inches.
- ☐ Handbrake moves to the center console.
- ☐ Manually operated and power-operated telescoping antennas of the past Sting Rays are gone, replaced by a 31-inch fixed antenna.
- ☐ Hardtop headliner is offered in black only.
- ☐ Passenger grab bar on dash top is removed.
- ☐ Functional louvers on side of fenders now have five slots instead of three.
- ☐ Seat belt buckles are changed to aluminum.

Specifications

Base Price: $4,388.75 Coupe, $4,240.75 Convertible
Chassis and Body Numbers: 194677S100001 through 194677S122940 (194377-Coupe)

I.D. Location: Hinge pillar cross brace under glove box.
Curb Weight: 3340 lbs.
Weight Distribution: 51/49
Turning Circle: 41.6 ft.
Wheelbase: 98 inches
Track, front: 57.6 inches, rear: 58.3 inches
Height: 49.8 inches

Length: 175.1 inches
Width: 69.6 inches
Steering Ratio: 20.2:1 std., 17.6:1 optional and w/power steering
Wheel Rim: 15 × 6JK
Standard Tire Size: 7.75 × 15

Identification Numbers

Engine Suffix: 327 c.i.: HE (manual), HH (A.I.R./California), HR (A.I.R./California/auto.), HD (S.H.P./A.I.R./California), HO (auto), HT (S.H.P.), HP (S.H.P./power steering/AC), KH (S.H.P./A.I.R./California/AC)

427 c.i.: IL (auto/manual), JC (tri-carb.), JE (S.H.P./tri-carb.), IT (heavy duty), IU (alum. heads), IM (A.I.R./California), JF (tri-carb./A.I.R./California), JH (alum. heads/A.I.R./California), IQ (auto.), JD (tri-carb/auto), IR (Auto/A.I.R./California), JG (auto/A.I.R./California/tri-carb), JA (S.H.P./tri-carb/A.I.R./California)

Note: HP—high performance, S.H.P.—special high performance, A.I.R.—air injector reactor.

Head Casting: All 327 c.i. engines.
Distributor: 1111117, 1111194, (300 hp.) 1111240 (430 hp.), 1111196, 1111157 (350 hp.), 1111258 (435 hp.), 1111247, 1111294 (390, 400 hp.)
Block Casting: 3892657 (327 c.i. engines)
3869942 (390, 400 hp.), 3904351 (435 hp., L-71/L-89)
Carburetor: Holley R3810A, R3814A (300, 350 hp.), R3811A R3815A (390 hp.), R3660A, R 3659A (400, 435 hp.), R3888A, R3659A, R3418A (400,430 HP/auto.)

Options

Factory No.	Item	Price
A01	Soft ray tinted glass, all windows	$15.80
A02	Soft ray tinted glass, windshield	10.55
A31	Electric power windows	57.95
A82	Headrests	42.15
A85	Shoulder belts (coupe only)	26.35

Factory No.	Item	Price
C07	Auxiliary hardtop	231.75
C08	Auxiliary hardtop vinyl covering	52.70
C48	Heater and defroster deletion for credit	97.85
C60	Air conditioning	412.90
F41	Front and rear suspension, special	36.90
G81	Positraction	42.15
J50	Power brakes	42.15
J56	Heavy duty brakes, special	342.30
K19	Air injection reactor	NC
K66	Transistorized ignition system	73.75
L36	427 c.i. engine, 390 hp.	200.15
L68	427 c.i. engine, 400 hp.	305.50
L71	427 c.i. engine, 435 hp.	437.10
L79	327 c.i. engine, 350 hp.	105.35
L88	427 c.i. engine, 430 hp.	947.90
L89	Aluminum heads for L71 option	368.65
M20	4-speed transmission	184.35
M21	4-speed close ratio transmission	184.35
M22	4-speed close ratio transmission, heavy duty	237.00
M35	Powerglide automatic transmission	194.35
N03	Gasoline tank, 36 gallon (coupe only)	198.05
N11	Off-road exhaust	36.90
N14	Side mount exhaust system	131.65
N36	Telescopic steering wheel	42.15
N40	Power steering	94.80
N89	Cast aluminum bolt-on wheels	262.30
P92	7.75×15 whitewall tires	31.35
Q81	7.75×15 Redline tires	46.65
U15	Speed warning indicator	10.55
U69	AM/FM radio	172.75

Colors

Factory Number	Exterior Color	Interior Color	Convertible Top
972	Ermine White	Black, Red, Saddle, Green, Bright Blue, Teal Blue, White	Teal Blue, Black, White
986	Silver Pearl	Black, White, Teal Blue	Teal Blue, Black, White
974	Rally Red	Black, White, Teal Blue	Teal Blue, Black, White
988	Marlboro Maroon	Black, White	Teal Blue, Black, White
984	Sunfire Yellow	Black, White	Teal Blue, Black, White
980	Elkhart Blue	Black, Teal Blue	Teal Blue, Black, White
977	Lynndale Blue	Black, White, Teal Blue	Teal Blue, Black, White
976	Marina Blue	Black, Bright Blue, White	Teal Blue, Black, White
983	Goodwood Green	Black, Silver, White, Green	Teal Blue, Black, White
900	Tuxedo Black	Black, Red, Saddle, Green, Bright Blue, Teal Blue, White	Teal Blue, Black, White

1968

Identification

- ☐ Introduction of the third generation of Corvettes.
- ☐ Standard wheel size increases to seven inches.
- ☐ Coupe features removable roof panels resulting in the term "T-top."
- ☐ Turbohydramatic automatic transmission is introduced.
- ☐ Rear window in coupes is removable.
- ☐ Battery moves from engine compartment to stowage area behind seats.
- ☐ Again, as in 1963, so many features were changed that it is impossible to detail all of them.

Specifications

Base Price: $4663.00 Coupe; $4320.00 Convertible
Chassis and Body Numbers: 194678S400001 through 194678S428566 (194378-Coupe)

I.D. Location: Hinge pillar cross brace under glove box.
Curb Weight: 3425 lbs.
Weight Distribution: 51/49
Turning Circle: 41.6 ft.
Wheelbase: 98 inches
Track, front: 58.3 inches, rear: 59 inches
Height: 47.8 inches
Length: 182.1 inches
Width: 69.2 inches

Steering Ratio: 20.2:1 std., 17.6:1 power steering
Wheel Rim: 15 × 7JK
Standard Tire Size: F70 × 15

Identification Numbers

Engine Suffix: 327 c.i. : HE (manual), HO (auto.), HP (power steering/AC), HT (S.H.P.)
427 c.i.:IL (high performance), IM (high performance/tri-carb), IO (high performance/auto/tri-carb), IQ (auto), IR (S.H.P./tri-carb), IT (heavy duty), IU (S.H.P./tri-carb/alum. heads.)

Note: S.H.P.—Special High Performance.

Options

Factory No.	Item	Price
A01	Soft ray tinted glass, all windows	$15.80
A31	Electric power windows	57.95
A82	Headrests	42.15
A85	Shoulder belts (coupe only)	26.35
C07	Auxiliary hardtop	231.75
C08	Auxiliary hardtop vinyl covering	52.70
C50	Rear window defroster	31.60
C60	Air conditioning	412.90
F41	Front and rear suspension, special	36.90
G81	Positraction	46.35
J50	Power brakes	42.15
J56	Heavy duty brakes	384.45
K66	Transistorized ignition system	73.75
L36	427 c.i. engine, 390 hp.	200.15
L68	427 c.i. engine, 400 hp.	305.50
L71	427 c.i. engine, 435 hp.	437.10
L79	327 c.i. engine, 350 hp.	105.35
L88	427 c.i. engine, 435 hp.	947.90
L89	Aluminum heads for L71 option	805.75
M20	4-speed transmission	184.35
M21	4-speed close ratio transmission	184.35
M22	4-speed close ratio transmission, heavy duty	263.30
M40	Turbohydramatic automatic transmission	226.45
N11	Off-road exhaust	36.90
N36	Telescopic steering wheel	42.15

Factory No.	Item	Price
N40	Power steering	94.80
P01	Wheel covers	57.95
PT6	F70×15 red stripe Nylon tires	31.30
PT7	F70×15 white stripe Nylon tires	31.30
UA6	Alarm system	26.35
U15	Speed warning indicator	10.55
U69	AM/FM radio	172.75
U79	AM/FM stereo radio	278.10

Colors

Factory Number	Exterior Color	Interior Color	Convertible Top
972	Polar White	Black, Red, Dark Blue, Medium Blue, Dark Orange, Gunmetal, Tobacco	
976	LeMans Blue	Black, Dark Blue, Medium Blue	
978	International Blue	Black, Dark Blue, Medium Blue	Black
974	Rally Red	Black, Red	White
988	Cordovan Maroon	Black	Beige
992	Corvette Bronze	Black, Tobacco, Dark Orange	*(All Models)*
983	British Green	Black	
984	Safari Yellow	Black	
986	Silverstone Silver	Black, Dark Blue, Gunmetal	
900	Tuxedo Black	Black, Red, Dark Blue, Medium Blue, Dark Orange, Gunmetal, Tobacco	

1969

Identification

- ☐ Standard wheel size increases to eight inches.
- ☐ Introduction of the 350 c.i. engine, replacing the faithful 327.
- ☐ Steering wheel diameter decreases from 16 to 15 inches.
- ☐ Introduction of the steering column lock.
- ☐ Map pocket added to passenger's side of dash.
- ☐ Sting Ray logo changes to one word: Stingray.
- ☐ Door lock buttons disappear in favor of an all-purpose outside door lock mechanism.

Specifications

Base Price: $4663.00 Coupe; $4402.00 Convertible
Chassis and Body Numbers: 194679S700001 through 194679S738762

I.D. Location: Hinge pillar cross brace under glove box.
Curb Weight: 3260 lbs.
Weight Distribution: 50/50

Turning Circle: 40 ft.
Wheelbase: 98 inches
Track, front 58.7 inches, rear 59.4 inches
Height: 47.9 inches
Length: 182.5 inches
Width: 69 inches
Steering Ratio: 20.2:1 std., 17.6:1 with power steering
Wheel Rim: 15 × 8JJ
Standard Tire Size: F70 × 15

Identification Numbers

Engine Suffix: 350 c.i.: HW (high performance), HX (high performance/AC), HY (manual), HZ (auto.)

427 c.i.: LL (auto), LM (high performance), LN (high performance/tri-carb/auto.), LO (heavy duty), LP (alum. heads), LQ (high performance/tri-carb), LR (S.H.P./tri-carb), LT (S.H.P./tri-carb/heavy duty clutch), LV (heavy duty/auto.), LW (alum. heads/auto.), LX (S.H.P./tri-carb/auto.)

Factory No.	Item	Price
A01	Soft ray tinted glass, all windows	$16.90
A31	Electric power windows	63.20
A85	Shoulder belts (coupe only)	42.15
C07	Auxiliary hardtop	252.80
C08	Auxiliary hardtop vinyl covering	57.95
C50	Rear window defroster	32.65
C60	Air conditioning	428.70
F41	Front and rear suspension, special	36.90
	Positraction	46.35
J50	Power brakes	42.15
K05	Engine block heater	10.55
K66	Transistorized ignition system	81.10
L36	427 c.i. engine, 390 hp.	221.20
L46	350 c.i. engines, 350 hp.	131.65
L68	427 c.i. engine, 400 hp.	326.55
L71	427 c.i. engine, 435 hp.	437.10
L89	427 c.i. engine, 435 hp.	832.05

Factory No.	Item	Price
M20	4-speed transmission	184.80
M21	4-speed close ratio transmission	184.80
M22	4-speed close ratio transmission, heavy duty	290.40
M40	Turbohydramatic automatic transmission	221.80
N14	Side mount exhaust system	147.45
N37	Tilt-telescopic steering wheel	84.30
N40	Power steering	105.35
P02	Wheel covers	57.95
PT6	F70×15 red stripe Nylon tires	31.30
PT7	F70×15 white stripe Nylon tires	31.30
TJ2	Front fender louver trim	21.10
UA6	Alarm system	26.35
U15	Speed warning indicator	11.60
U69	AM/FM radio	172.45
U79	AM/FM stereo radio	278.10

Colors

Factory Number	Exterior Color	Interior Color	Convertible Top
972	Can-Am White	Black, Bright Blue, Red, Green, Gunmetal, Saddle	
976	LeMans Blue	Bright Blue, Black	
974	Monza Red	Black, Red, Saddle	
988	Burgundy	Black, Saddle	Black
990	Monaco Orange	Black	White
983	Fathom Green	Black, Saddle, Green	Beige
984	Daytona Yellow	Black	*(All*
980	Riverside Gold	Black	*Models)*
986	Cortez Silver	Black, Green, Red, Saddle, Bright Blue, Gunmetal	
900	Tuxedo Black	Black, Bright Blue, Red, Green, Gunmetal, Saddle	

1970

Identification

- ☐ Introduction of the 454 c.i. engine, replacing the 427 engine.
- ☐ LT-1 350 c.i. engine offered. This is the first new small-block engine offered in years.
- ☐ Exhaust outlets are now square.
- ☐ Standard equipment now includes tinted glass, four-speed transmission or automatic transmission and Positraction.
- ☐ Amber parking light of new design offered.

Specifications

Base Price: $5,192.00 Coupe; $4849.00 Convertible.
Chassis and Body Numbers: 194670S400001 through 194670S417316

I.D. Location: Left windshield pillar.
Curb Weight: 3720 lbs.
Weight Distribution: 53/47
Turning Circle: 39 ft.
Wheelbase: 98 inches

Track, front: 58.7 inches, rear: 59.4 inches
Height: 47.5 inches
Length: 182.5 inches
Width: 69 inches
Steering Ratio: 20.2:1 std., 17.6:1 with power steering
Wheel Rim: 15 × 8 JJ
Standard Tire Size: F70 × 15

Identification Numbers

Engine Suffix: 350 c.i. : CTL (manual), CTM (auto.), CTN (high performance), CTQ (high performance/trans ign./AC), CTO (high performance/AC), CTP (high performance/trans. ign.), CTR (S.H.P.), CTU (S.H.P./trans. ign.), CTV (S.H.P./trans ign./manual)

454 c.i.: CGW (high performance/auto.), CZU (high performance), CZL (heavy duty), CZN (heavy duty/auto.), CRI (high performance/trans. ign.)

Options

Factory No.	Item	Price
A31	Electric power windows	63.20
A85	Shoulder belts (coupe only)	42.15
C07	Auxiliary hardtop	273.85
C08	Auxiliary hardtop vinyl covering	63.20
C50	Rear window defroster	36.90
C60	Air conditioning	447.65
	Positraction	12.65
J50	Power brakes	47.40
L46	350 c.i. engines, 350 hp.	158.00
LS5	454 c.i. engines, 390 hp.	289.65
LS7	454 c.i. engine, 460 hp.	Refer to Note
LT1	350 c.i. engine, 370 hp.	447.60
M21	4-speed close ratio transmission	N/C
M22	4-speed close ratio transmission, heavy duty	95.00
M40	Turbohydramatic automatic transmission	N/C
N37	Tilt-telescopic steering wheel	84.30
N40	Power steering	105.35

P01	Wheel covers	57.95
PT7	F70×15 white stripe Nylon tires	31.30
PU9	F70×15 white letter Nylon tires	33.15
T60	Heavy duty battery	15.80
UA6	Alarm system	31.60
U69	AM/FM radio	172.75
U79	AM/FM stereo radio	278.10

Note: Option LS7, 460 hp. 454 c.i. engine, was available for approximately $2,900.00. It was sold mainly to race teams.

Colors

Factory Number	Exterior Color	Interior Color	Convertible Top
10	Classic White	Black, Blue, Red, Green, Saddle, Brown	
27	Bridgehampton Blue	Black, Blue	
26	Mulsanne Blue	Black, Blue	
72	Monza Red	Black, Red, Saddle, Brown	
77	Marlboro Maroon	Black, Saddle, Brown	Black, White
62	Ontario Orange	Black	*(All Models)*
44	Donneybrooke Green	Black, Green, Saddle, Brown	
51	Daytona Yellow	Black, Green	
15	Laguna Gray	Black, Blue, Red, Green, Saddle, Brown	
14	Cortez Silver	Black, Blue, Red, Green, Saddle, Brown	

1971

Identification

- ☐ Few changes took place between the 1970 and 1971 models. Many of the photos used in the 1970 promotional literature were used again in the 1971 literature!
- ☐ LS6 option replaces the LS7 option, which was only available to racers. LS6 option included aluminum heads.
- ☐ ZR1 engine option included these extra items: heavy-duty power brakes, heavy-duty four-speed transmission, aluminum radiator, special springs and shocks, special front stabilizer, and rear wheel spindle strut shafts.

Specifications

Base Price: $5496.00 Coupe; $5259.00 Convertible
Chassis and Body Numbers: 194671S100001 through
                            194671S12180 (194371-Coupe)

I.D. Location: Left windshield pillar.
Curb Weight: 3593 lbs.
Weight Distribution: 49/51
Turning Circle: 39 ft.
Wheelbase: 98 inches
Track, front: 58.7 inches, rear: 59.4 inches
Height: 74.9 inches
Length: 182.5 inches
Width: 69 inches
Steering Ratio: 20.2:1 std., 17.6:1 with power steering

Wheel Rim: 15 × 8JJ
Standard Tire Size: F70 × 15

Identification Numbers

Engine Suffix: 350 c.i.: CJL (270 hp., manual), CJT (270 hp., auto.), CGZ (330 hp., manual), CGY (330 hp., auto.)
454 c.i.: CPJ (365 hp., auto.), CPH (365 hp., manual), CPX (425 hp., auto.), CPW (425 hp., manual)

Options

Factory No.	*Item*	*Price*
A31	Electric power windows	79.00
A85	Shoulder belts (coupe only)	42.00
C07	Auxiliary hardtop	274.00
C08	Auxiliary hardtop vinyl covering	63.00
C50	Rear window defroster	42.00
C60	Air conditioning	459.00
	Positraction, optional ratios	13.00
J50	Power brakes	47.00
LS5	454 c.i. engine, 365 hp.	295.00
LS6	454 c.i. engine, 425 hp.	1221.00
LT1	350 c.i. engine, 330 hp.	483.00
ZR1	350 c.i. engine, 330 hp.	1010.00
ZR2	454 c.i. engine, 425 hp.	1747.00
M21	4-speed close ratio transmission	N/C
M22	4-speed close ratio transmission, heavy duty	100.00
M40	Turbohydramatic automatic transmission	N/C
N37	Tilt-telescopic steering wheel	84.30
N40	Power steering	115.90
P02	Wheel covers	63.00
PT7	F70×15 white stripe Nylon tires	28.00
PU9	F70×15 white letter Nylon tires	42.00
T60	Heavy duty battery	15.80
U69	AM/FM radio	178.00
U79	AM/FM stereo radio	283.00

Note: Option M40, Turbohydramatic transmission, was available with high performance engines for $100.00.

Colors

Factory Number	Exterior Color	Interior Color	Convertible Top
972 (10)	Classic White	Black, Dark Blue, Red, Dark Green, Saddle	Black, White
979 (27)	Bridgehampton Blue	Black, Dark Blue	Black, White
976 (26)	Mulsanne Blue	Black, Dark Blue	Black, White
973 (76)	Millie Miglia Red	Black, Red	Black, White
987 (97)	Ontario Orange	Black, Dark Green, Saddle	Black, White
983 (48)	Brands Hatch Green	Black, Dark Green	Black, White
912 (52)	Sunflower Yellow	Black, Dark Green, Saddle	Black, White
989 (91)	War Bonnet Yellow	Black, Dark Green, Saddle	Black, White
988 (98)	Steel Cities Grey	Black, Saddle	Black, White
905 (13)	Nevada Silver	Black, Dark Blue, Red, Dark Green	Black, White

1972

Identification

- ☐ Again, few changes took place between the 1971 and 1972 models.
- ☐ Anti-theft alarm system now standard equipment.
- ☐ Last year for the removable rear window in the coupes.

Specifications

Base Price: $5533 Coupe; $5296 Convertible
Chassis and Body Numbers: 1Z67K2S500001 through 1Z67K2S527004

I. D. Location: Left windshield pillar.
Curb Weight: 3356 lbs.
Weight Distribution: 49/51
Turning Circle: 39 ft.
Wheelbase: 98 inches
Track, front: 58.7 inches, rear: 59.4 inches
Height: 47.9 inches
Length: 182.5 inches
Width: 69 inches
Steering Ratio: 20.2:1 std., 17.6:1 optional and with power steering
Wheel Rim: 15 × 8
Standard Tire Size: F70 × 15

Identification Numbers

Engine Suffix: 350 c.i.: CDH (manual/NB2), CDJ (auto/NB2), CKW (manual), CKX (auto), CKY (manual/LT-1), CKZ (heavy duty/ manual/LT-1), CRT (manual/LT-1/ARO)

454 c.i.: CPH (manual), CPJ (auto), CSR (AR). CSS (AR)

Note: NB2: California emissions; AR: Air injection reactor

Options

Factory No.	Item	Price
A31	Electric power windows	85.35
A85	Shoulder belts (coupe only)	26.35
C07	Auxiliary hardtop	273.85
C08	Auxiliary hardtop vinyl covering	63.00
C50	Rear window defroster	42.15
C60	Air conditioning	464.50
	Positraction, optional ratios	12.65
J50	Power brakes	47.40
LS5	454 c.i. engines, 270 hp.	294.90
LT1	350 c.i. engine, 255 hp.	483.45
ZR1	350 c.i. engine, 255 hp.	1010.05
M21	4-speed close ratio transmission	N/C
M40	Turbohydramatic automatic transmission	N/C
N37	Tilt-telescopic steering wheel	84.30
N40	Power steering	115.90
P02	Wheel covers	63.20

Factory No.	Item	Price
PT7	F70×15 white stripe Nylon tires	30.35
PU9	F70×15 white letter Nylon tires	43.65
T60	Heavy duty battery	15.80
U69	AM/FM radio	178.00
U79	AM/FM stereo radio	283.35

Note: Option LT1 came equipped with option C60 only in 1972. Normally the LT1 option came with a 6500 rpm tachometer; however, these models came with a 5600 rpm tachometer in the hopes that this would prevent the driver from over-revving the engine and allowing the belts to slip from the pulleys.

Colors

Factory Number	Exterior Color	Interior Color	Convertible Top
972	Classic White	Black, Blue, Red, Saddle	Black, White
945	Byrar Blue	Black	Black, White
979	Targa Blue	Black, Blue	Black, White
973	Millie Miglia Red	Black, Red, Saddle	Black, White
987	Ontario Orange	Black, Saddle	Black, White
946	Elkhart Green	Black, Saddle	Black, White
912	Sunflower Yellow	Black, Saddle	Black, White
989	War Bonnet Yellow	Black, Saddle	Black, White
988	Steel Cities Gray	Black, Red, Saddle	Black, White
924	Pewter Silver	Black, Blue, Red, Saddle	Black, White

1973

Identification

☐ Safety steel beam installed in doors.
☐ Federally inspired impact-absorbing front bumpers mark the biggest visual difference between this model and the previous four years.
☐ Body/chassis mounts were greatly improved, which led to many older third-generation Corvettes being converted to their use also.
☐ First model since 1967 to have nonremovable rear window.
☐ Anti-theft system becomes standard.

Specifications

Base Price: $5561.50 Coupe; $5398.50 Convertible
Chassis and Body Numbers: 1Z67J3S400001 through 1Z67J3S438464

I. D. Location: Left windshield pillar.
Curb Weight: 3725 lbs.
Weight Distribution: 52/48
Turning Circle: 38.6 ft.
Wheelbase: 98 inches
Track, front: 58.7 inches, rear: 59.5 inches
Height: 47.8 inches
Length: 184.7 inches
Width: 69 inches

Steering Ratio: 20.2:1 std., 17.6:1 optional and with power steering
Wheel Rim: 15 × 8
Standard Tire Size: GR70 × 15

Identification Numbers

Engine Suffix: 350 c.i.: CLA (auto/L-48), CLB (manual/NB2/L-48), CLC (auto/NB2/L-48), CLD (auto/L-82), CLH (auto/NB2/L-82), CLR (manual/L-82), CLS (manual/NB2/L-82), CKZ (manual/L-48)

454 c.i.: CWM (manual/L-54), CWR (auto/L-54), CWS (auto/NB2/L-54), CWT (manual/NB2/L-54)

Note: NB2: California emissions

Options

Factory No.	Item	Price
A31	Electric power windows	83.00
A85	Shoulder belts (coupe only)	41.00
C07	Auxiliary hardtop	267.00
C08	Auxiliary hardtop vinyl covering	62.00
C50	Rear window defroster	41.00
C60	Air conditioning	452.00
	Positraction, optional ratios	12.00
J50	Power brakes	46.00
L82	350 c.i. engine, 250 hp.	299.00
LS4	454 c.i. engine, 275 hp.	250.00
M21	4-speed close ratio transmission	N/C
M40	Turbohydramatic automatic transmission	N/C
N37	Tilt-telescopic steering wheel	82.00
N40	Power steering	113.00
P02	Wheel covers	62.00
QRM	GR70×15 white stripe steel-belted radial tires	32.00
QRZ	GR70×15 white letter steel-belted radial tires	45.00
T60	Heavy duty battery	15.00
U58	AM/FM stereo radio	276.00
U69	AM/FM radio	173.00
UF1	Map light	5.00
YJ8	Cast aluminum wheels	175.00
Z07	Off-road suspension and brake package	369.00

Note: Option YJ8, cast aluminum wheels, were never made available to the public. Approximately 800 sets were distributed by a California company which was producing them for GM. The wheels did not meet quality requirements and, therefore, were not officially released to the public.

Colors

Factory Number	Exterior Color	Interior Color	Convertible Top
910	Classic White	Black, Midnight Blue, Dark Red, Medium Saddle, Dark Saddle	Black White
922	Medium Blue	Black, Midnight Blue, Medium Saddle	Black White
927	Dark Blue	Black, Midnight Blue, Dark Red, Medium Saddle	Black White
945	Blue-Green	Black, Dark Red, Medium Saddle, Dark Saddle	Black White
980	Orange	Black, Medium Saddle	Black White
976	Millie Miglia Red	Black, Midnight Blue, Dark Red, Medium Saddle, Dark Saddle	Black White
947	Elkhart Green	Black, Medium Saddle	Black White
952	Yellow	Black, Midnight Blue, Dark Saddle	Black White
953	Yellow (Metallic)	Black, Midnight Blue	Black White
914	Silver	Black, Midnight Blue, Dark Red, Medium Saddle, Dark Saddle	Black White

1974

Identification

- ☐ Federally regulated impact-absorbing rear bumpers are introduced. Urethane material is painted and tends to fade.
- ☐ Anti-theft system is moved from the rear to the driver's side fender panel.
- ☐ Shoulder belts are integrated with the lap belts.
- ☐ This the last year for true dual exhaust. Emissions control makes this impossible in the future when utilizing a catalytic converter, although exhaust does branch out into two tailpipes from the converter, giving a dual exhaust impression.
- ☐ This is the last year for the 454 c.i. engine.

Specifications

Base Price: $6001.50 Coupe; $5765.50 Convertible
Chassis and Body Numbers: 1Z67J4S400001 through 1Z267J4S437502

I. D. Location: Left windshield pillar.
Curb Weight: 3492 lbs.
Weight Distribution: 48/52
Turning Circle: 38.6 ft.
Wheelbase: 98 inches
Track, front: 58.7 inches, rear: 59.5 inches
Height: 47.7 inches
Length: 185.5 inches

Width: 69 inches
Steering Ratio: 20.2:1 std., 17.6:1 optional and with power steering
Wheel Rim: 15 × 8
Standard Tire Size: GR70 × 15

Identification Numbers

Engine Suffix: 350 c.i.: CLA (auto/L-48), CLB (manual/NB2/L-48), CLC (auto/NB2/L-48), CLD (auto/L-82), CLR (manual/L-82), CKZ (manual/L-48)

454 c.i.: CWM (manual/L-54), CWR (auto/L-54), CWS (auto/NB2/L-54)

Note: NB2: California emissions

Options

Factory No.	*Item*	*Price*
A31	Electric power windows	$86.00
A85	Shoulder belts (coupe only)	41.00
C07	Auxiliary hardtop	267.00
C08	Vinyl covering hardtop	329.00
C50	Rear window defroster	43.00
C60	Air conditioning	467.00
FE7	Gymkhana suspension	7.00
	Positraction, optional ratios	12.00
J50	Power brakes	49.00
L82	350 c.i. engine, 250 hp.	299.00
LS4	454 c.i. engine, 270 hp.	250.00
M21	4-speed close ratio transmission	N/C
M40	Turbohydramatic automatic transmission	N/C
N37	Tilt-telescopic steering wheel	82.00
N41	Power steering	117.00
QRM	GR70×15 white stripe steel-belted radial tires	32.00
QRZ	GR70×15 white letter steel-belted radial tires	45.00
U05	Dual horns	4.00
U58	AM/FM stereo radio	276.00
U69	AM/FM radio	173.00
UA1	Heavy duty battery	15.00
UF1	Map light	5.00
Z07	Off-road suspension and brake package	400.00

Colors

Factory Number	Exterior Color	Interior Color	Convertible Top
910	Classic White	Black, Dark Blue, Dark Red, Neutral, Saddle, Silver	Black, White
922	Corvette Medium Blue	Black, Dark Blue, Silver	Black, White
980	Corvette Orange	Black, Neutral, Saddle, Silver	Black, White
976	Millie Miglia Red	Black, Dark Red, Neutral, Saddle, Silver	Black, White
974	Medium Red	Black, Dark Red, Neutral, Saddle, Silver	Black, White
948	Dark Green	Black, Neutral, Saddle, Silver	Black, White
956	Bright Yellow	Black, Neutral, Saddle, Silver	Black, White
968	Dark Brown	Black, Neutral, Saddle, Silver	Black, White
917	Corvette Gray	Black, Dark Blue, Dark Red, Neutral, Saddle, Silver	Black, White
914	Silver Mist	Black, Dark Blue, Dark Red, Saddle, Silver	Black, White

1975

Identification

☐ Introduction of the catalytic converter.
☐ Introduction of Delco's HEI ignition system.
☐ Last Corvette convertible is built in July 1975.
☐ Black bumper pads added to the front and rear bumpers.
☐ Introduction of the kilometer-per-hour speedometer face.
☐ Vents in the rear deck disappear.

Specifications

Base Price: $6,810.00 Coupe; $6550.00 Convertible
Chassis and Body Numbers: 1Z67J5S40001 through 1Z67J5S438465
I. D. Location: Left windshield pillar.
Curb Weight: 3660 lbs.
Weight Distribution: 48/52
Turning Circle: 38.6 ft.
Wheelbase: 98 inches
Track, front: 58.7 inches, rear: 59.5 inches
Height: 48.1 inches
Length: 185.2 inches
Width: 69 inches
Steering Ratio: 20.2:1 std., 17.6:1 optional and with power steering
Wheel Rim: 15 × 8
Standard Tire Size: GR70 × 15

Identification Numbers

Engine Suffix: CRJ (manual), CRK (auto), CRL (high performance L-82/manual) CRM (high performance L-82/auto), CVA (manual), CUB (manual), CUD (high performance L-82/manual), CUT (high performance L-82/manual)

Options

Factory No.	Item	Price
A31	Electric power windows	93.00
A85	Shoulder belts (coupe only)	41.00
C07	Auxiliary hardtop	267.00
C08	Vinyl covered hardtop	350.00
C50	Rear window defroster	46.00
C60	Air conditioning	490.00
FE7	Gymkhana suspension	7.00
	Positraction, optional ratios	12.00
J50	Power brakes	50.00
L82	350 c.i. engine, 205 hp.	336.00
M21	4-speed close ratio transmission	N/C
M40	Turbohydramatic automatic transmission	N/C
N37	Tilt-telescopic steering wheel	82.00
N41	Power steering	129.00
QRM	GR70×15 white stripe steel-belted radial tires	35.00
QRZ	GR70×15 white letter steel-belted radial tires	48.00
U05	Dual horns	4.00
U58	AM/FM stereo radio	284.00
U69	AM/FM radio	178.00
UA1	Heavy duty battery	15.00
UF1	Map light	5.00
Z07	Off-road suspension and brake package	400.00

Note: Option M40, Turbohydramatic transmission, was available with option L82 for $120.00.

Colors

Factory Number	Exterior Color	Interior Color	Convertible Top
10	Classic White	Black, Dark Blue, Dark Red, Neutral, Medium Saddle, Silver	Black, White
22	Bright Blue	Black, Dark Blue, Silver	Black, White
27	Steel Blue	Black, Dark Blue, Silver	Black, White
70	Orange Flame	Black, Neutral, Medium Saddle	Black, White
76	Millie Miglia Red	Black, Dark Red, Neutral, Medium Saddle, Silver	Black, White
74	Dark Red	Black, Dark Red, Neutral, Medium Saddle, Silver	Black, White
42	Bright Green	Black, Neutral, Medium Saddle, Silver	Black, White
56	Bright Yellow	Black, Neutral, Medium Saddle	Black, White
67	Medium Saddle	Black, Neutral, Medium Saddle	Black, White
13	Silver	Black, Dark Blue, Dark Red, Medium Saddle, Silver	Black, White

1976

Identification

- ☐ Belly pan changes from fiberglass to steel.
- ☐ Some late 1976 vehicles are delivered with 1977 insignias and interiors.
- ☐ Early aluminum wheels were recalled but a replacement, made by Kelsey-Hayes, was available later. Only four wheels were provided, with the spare constructed of steel.
- ☐ Introduction of Delco's New Freedom battery as standard equipment.
- ☐ New sport steering wheel is introduced but enthusiasts recognize it as the same one used in the Vega. The new wheel disappears under waves of protest by the next year.

Specifications

Base Price: $7605.00
Chassis and Body Numbers: 1Z37L6S400001
                         through 1Z37L6S446558

I. D. Location: Left windshield pillar.
Curb Weight: 3608 lbs.
Weight Distribution: 49/51
Turning Circle: 38.6 ft.
Wheelbase: 98 inches
Track, front: 58.7 inches, rear: 59.5 inches
Height: 48 inches

Length: 185.2 inches
Width: 69 inches
Steering Ratio: 20.2:1 std., 17.6:1 optional and with power steering
Wheel Rim: 15 × 8
Standard Tire Size: GR70 × 15

Identification Numbers
Engine Suffix: CHC, CHR, CKC, CLM, CLR, CLS

Options

Factory No.	Item	Price
A31	Electric power windows	$107.00
C49	Rear window defogger	78.00
C60	Air conditioning	523.00
FE7	Gymkhana suspension	35.00
	Positraction, optional ratios	13.00
J50	Power brakes	59.00
L82	350 c.i. engine, 210 hp.	481.00
M21	4-speed close ratio transmission	N/C
M40	Turbohydramatic automatic transmission	N/C
N37	Tilt-telescopic steering wheel	95.00
N40	Power steering	151.00
QRM	GR70×15 white stripe steel-belted radial tires	37.00
QRZ	GR70×15 white letter steel-belted radial tires	51.00
U58	AM/FM stereo radio	281.00
U69	AM/FM radio	187.00
UA1	Heavy duty battery	16.00
UF1	Map light	10.00
YJ8	Aluminum wheels	299.00

Note: Option M40, Turbohydramatic transmission, was available with option L82 for $134.00.

Colors

Factory Number	Exterior Color	Interior Color
10	Classic White	Black, Dark Blue, Blue Green, Firethorn, Buckskin, Smoked Gray, White
22	Bright Blue	Black, Smoked Gray

Factory	Exterior Color	Interior Color
70	Orange Flame	Black, Dark Blue, Buckskin
72	Red	Black, Fire Thorn, Buckskin, Smoked Gray, White
33	Dark Green	Black, Blue Green, Buck Skin, Smoked Gray, White
56	Bright Yellow	Black, Dark Blue
64	Buckskin	Black, Dark Blue, Fire Thorn, Buckskin, White
37	Mahogany	Black, Firethorn, Buckskin, Smoked Gray, White
69	Dark Brown	Black, Dark Blue, Buckskin, White
13	Silver	Black, Blue Green, Fire Thorn, Buckskin, Smoked Gray, White

1977

Identification

- ☐ Anti-theft system is moved to the ignition lock.
- ☐ Glass roof panels are introduced as an option for the T-top.
- ☐ Leather seats are standard equipment.
- ☐ Headlight dimmer, windshield washer and wiper are incorporated on one stalk from the steering column.
- ☐ Introduction of cruise control.
- ☐ Steering wheel moved two inches closer to the dash.
- ☐ Sunshades now move to the side windows.
- ☐ Windshield trim changes to non-glare black.
- ☐ Rear view mirror attaches to windshield.
- ☐ Center console is redesigned to accommodate standard GM corporation radios and new heater and air conditioning controls.

Specifications

Base Price: $8,647.00
Chassis and Body Numbers: 1Z37L7S400001
through 1Z37L7S449213

I. D. Location: Left windshield pillar.
Curb Weight: 3595 lbs.
Weight Distribution: 48/52
Turning Circle: 38.6 ft.
Wheelbase: 98 inches

Track, front: 58.7 inches, rear: 59.5 inches
Height: 48 inches
Length: 185.2 inches
Width: 69 inches
Steering Ratio: 17.6:1
Wheel Rim: 15 × 8
Standard Tire Size: GR70 × 15

Identification Numbers
Engine Suffix: CLA, CLB, CLC, CLD, CLF, CKZ

Options

Factory No.	Item	Price
A31	Power windows	$116.00
B32	Color coordinated floormats	22.00
C49	Rear window defogger	84.00
C60	Air conditioning	553.00
D35	Sport mirrors	36.00
FE7	Gymkhana suspension	38.00
G95	Positraction, optional ratios	14.00
K30	Cruise control	88.00
L82	350 c.i. engine, 210 hp.	495.00
M21	4-speed close ratio transmission	N/C
M40	Turbohydramatic automatic transmission	N/C
N37	Tilt-telescopic steering wheel	165.00
QRZ	GR70×15 white letter steel-belted radial tires	57.00
UA1	Heavy duty battery	17.00
U58	AM/FM stereo radio	281.00
U69	AM/FM radio	187.00
UM2	AM/FM stereo radio with tape system	414.00
V54	Roof panel luggage rack	73.00
YJ8	Aluminum wheels	321.00
ZN1	Trailer package	83.00
ZX2	Convenience group	22.00

Note: Additional standard equipment included power brakes, power steering and leather interior. Option M40, Turbohydramatic transmission, was available with option L82 for $146.00.

Colors

Factory Number	Exterior Color	Interior Color
10	Classic White	Black, Blue, Red, Buckskin, Smoked Gray, Brown, White
26	Corvette Light Blue	Black, Smoked Gray, White
28	Corvette Dark Blue	Black, Blue, Buckskin, Smoked Gray, White
66	Corvette Orange	Black, Buckskin, Brown
72	Medium Red	Black, Red, Buckskin, Smoked Gray, White
83	Corvette Dark Red	Black, Buckskin, Smoked Gray
52	Corvette Yellow	Black, Brown
80	Corvette Tan	Black, Red, Buckskin, Brown, White
13	Silver	Black, Blue, Red, Smoked Gray, White
19	Black	Black, Red, Buckskin, Smoked Gray, White

1978

Identification

- ☐ Two special models are offered: the special edition Pace Car and the 25th Anniversary model.
- ☐ Interior features numerous changes: glove box reappears, removable armrests, new speedometer and tachometer, windshield wiper and washer controls return to dash, and the anti-theft system incorporates the removable roof panels.
- ☐ A larger rear window appears.

Specifications

Base Price: $9,352.00 (standard coupe), $13,653.21 (Pace Car Limited Edition)
Chassis and Body Numbers: 1Z87L8S400001 through 1Z87L8S440224; Pace Car 1Z87L8S900001 through 906502

I. D. Location: Left windshield pillar.
Curb Weight: 3495 lbs.
Weight Distribution: 47/53
Turning Circle: 38.6 ft.
Wheelbase: 98 inches
Track, front: 58.7 inches, rear: 59.5 inches
Height: 48 inches
Length: 185.2 inches
Width: 69 inches
Steering Ratio: 17.6:1

Wheel Rim: 15 × 8
Standard Tire Size: P225/70R15

Identification Numbers
Engine Suffix: CHW, CLM, CLR, CLS, CMR, CMS

Options

Factory No.	*Item*	*Price*
A31	Power windows	$130.00
AU3	Power door locks	120.00
B2Z	Silver anniversary paint scheme	399.00
CC1	Removable glass roof panels	349.00
C49	Rear window defogger	95.00
C60	Air conditioning	605.00
D35	Sport mirrors	40.00
FE7	Gymkhana suspension	41.00
G95	Positraction, optional ratios	15.00
K30	Cruise control	99.00
L82	350 c.i. engine, 220 hp.	525.00
M21	4-speed close ratio transmission	N/C
MX1	Turbohydramatic automatic transmission	N/C
N37	Tilt-telescopic steering wheel	175.00
QBS	P225/60R15 white letter steel-belted radial tires	216.32
QGR	P225/70R15 white letter steel-belted radial tires	51.00
UA1	Heavy duty battery	18.00
UM2	AM/FM stereo radio with tape system	419.00
UP6	AM/FM radio with CB system	638.00
U58	AM/FM stereo radio	286.00
U69	AM/FM radio	199.00
U75	Power antenna	49.00
U81	Dual rear speakers	49.00
YJ8	Aluminum wheels	340.00
ZN1	Trailer package	89.00
ZX2	Convenience group	84.00

Note: Pace Car base price included options A31, AU3, CC1, C49, C60, D35, N37, QBS, UA1, UM2, U75, U81, YJ8 and ZX2. The Silver Anniversary Special Edition was light silver on top and dark silver on the bottom. Mandatory options included D35 and YJ8.

Colors

Factory Number	Exterior Color	Interior Color
10	Classic White	Black, Dark Blue, Red, Light Beige, Mahogany, Oyster
26	Corvette Light Blue	Dark Blue
83	Corvette Dark Blue	Dark Blue, Light Beige, Oyster
72	Corvette Red	Black, Red, Light Beige, Oyster
52	Corvette Yellow	Black, Oyster
59	Corvette Light Beige	Black, Dark Blue, Light Beige, Mahogany
82	Corvette Mahogany	Black, Light Beige, Mahogany, Oyster
89	Corvette Dark Brown	Dark Blue, Light Beige, Oyster
13	Silver	Black, Dark Blue, Red, Mahogany
13	Silver Anniversary	Black, Red
19	Black	Black, Red, Light Beige, Mahogany, Oyster

1979

Identification

- ☐ Flatter folding bucket seats.
- ☐ Front air dam and rear spoiler standard equipment.
- ☐ Automatic transmission Corvettes now utilize 3.55:1 rear end ratio replacing 3.08:1 ratio.
- ☐ New dual snorkel air induction air cleaner.
- ☐ Halogen lamps standard on high beams.
- ☐ Introduction of steering column mounted anti-theft ignition lock.

Specifications

Base Price: $12,313.23
Chassis and Body Numbers: 1Z87895400001 through S453807
I.D. Location: Left windshield pillar.
Curb Weight: 3655 lbs.
Weight Distribution: 47.5/52.5
Turning Circle: 38.6 ft.
Wheelbase: 98 inches
Track, front: 58.7 inches, rear: 59.5 inches
Height: 48 inches
Length: 185.3 inches
Width: 69 inches
Steering Ratio: 17.6:1
Wheel Rim: 15 × 8
Standard Tire Size: P225/70R15

Identification Numbers
Engine Suffix: ZAB, ZAA, ZAC, ZAD, ZBB, ZBA

Options

Factory No.	Item	Price
A31	Power windows	$141.00
CC1	Roof panels	365.00
C49	Rear window defogger	102.00
C60	Air conditioning	635.00
D35	Sport mirrors	45.00
F51	Heavy Duty Shock Absorbers, Front & Rear	33.00
FE7	Gymkhana suspension	49.00
G95	Special Highway Ratio Rear Axles	19.00
K30	Cruise Control	113.00
L48	195 hp, 350 c.i. Engine	N/C
L82	225 hp, 350 c.i. Engine	565.00
M21	4-Speed Close Ratio Transmission	N/C
MM4	4-Speed Transmission	N/C
MX1	Turbohydramatic Transmission	N/C
N90	Aluminum Wheels	380.00
N37	Tilt-telescopic Steering Wheel	190.00
NA5	Emission Equipment	N/C
NA6	Emission Equipment, High Altitude	35.00
QBS	P225/60R15 Aramid Belted Radial Tires	226.00
QGR	P225/70R15 Steel Belted Radial Tires, White Letter	54.00
QGQ	P225/70R15 Steel Belted Radial Tires, Blackwall	N/C
UA1	Heavy Duty Battery	21.00
U58	AM/FM Stereo Radio	90.00
UM2	AM/FM Stereo Radio with Tape System	228.00
UN3	AM/FM Stereo Radio with Cassette Tape System	234.00
UP6	AM/FM Stereo Radio with CB Radio and Power Antenna	439.00
U75	Power Antenna	52.00
U81	Dual Rear Speakers	52.00
YF5	California Emission Requirements	83.00
ZN1	Trailer Package	98.00
ZQ2	Power Door Locks and Windows	272.00
ZX2	Convenience Group	94.00

Colors

Factory Number	Exterior Color	Interior Color
10	White	Black, Medium Red, Dark Blue, Light Doeskin, Dark Brown, Dark Green, Oyster White
13	Silver Metallic	Black, Medium Red, Dark Blue, Dark Green, Oyster White
83	Dark Blue Metallic	Black, Medium Red, Dark Blue, Light Doeskin, Oyster White
45	Frost Green	Black, Dark Green, Oyster White
52	Yellow	Black, Light Doeskin, Dark Brown, Oyster White
59	Frost Beige	Black, Medium Red, Dark Blue, Light Doeskin, Dark Brown, Dark Green
28	Frost Blue	Black, Dark Blue, Oyster White
72	Red	Black, Medium Red, Light Doeskin, Oyster White
58	Dark Green Metallic	Black, Light Doeskin, Dark Green
19	Black	Black, Medium Red, Light Doeskin, Oyster White

Two-Tone Combinations

Factory Number	Exterior Color		Interior Color
10	Upper	White	Black, Oyster White
	Lower	Oyster	
72	Upper	Red	Black, Medium Red
	Lower	Dark Red	
28	Upper	Frost Blue	Dark Blue
	Lower	Medium Blue	
59	Upper	Frost Beige	Light Doeskin, Dark Brown
	Lower	Medium Beige	
45	Upper	Frost Green	Dark Green
	Lower	Medium Green	

1980

Identification

- ☐ Front air dam and rear spoiler redesigned and molded in instead of bolted on.
- ☐ New deep-set grille with integral parking lamps.
- ☐ Automatic side corner lights are activated with main headlights or turn signals.
- ☐ New design of Corvette flags/badges.
- ☐ Additional applications of lightweight materials and technology.
- ☐ Thinner window glass, hood, and door skins.
- ☐ T-top roof panels constructed from lightweight low-density fiberglass.
- ☐ Third-member differential housing and intake manifold constructed of cast aluminum.
- ☐ New gearing in the four-speed transmissions.
- ☐ New torque converter in automatic transmission.

Specifications

Base Price: $13,140.00
Chassis and Body Numbers: 1Z878A S400001 through S440614
I.D. Location: Left windshield pillar.
Curb Weight: 3345 lbs.
Weight Distribution: 47.6/52.4
Turning Circle: 41.3 feet
Wheelbase: 98 inches

Track, front: 58.7 inches, rear: 59.5 inches
Height: 48 inches
Length: 185.3 inches
Width: 69 inches
Steering Ratio: 17.6:1
Wheel Rim: 15 × 8
Standard Tire Size: P225/70R15

Identification Numbers
Engine Suffix: ZAC, ZAK, ZAM, ZBC, ZBD

Options

Factory No.	Item	Price
AU3	Power Door Locks, Electric	$140.00
C49	Rear Window Defogger	109.00
CC1	Roof Panels	391.00
F51	Heavy Duty Shock Absorbers, Front & Rear	35.00
FE7	Gymkhana Suspension	55.00
K30	Cruise Control	123.00
L48	190 hp, 350 c.i. Engine	N/C
L82	230 hp, 350 c.i. Engine	595.00
LG4	180 hp, 305 c.i. Engine	(Credit) 50.00
MM4	4-Speed Transmission	N/C
MX1	Turbohydramatic Transmission	N/C
N90	Aluminum Wheels	407.00
NA5	Emission Equipment	N/C
QGQ	P225/70R15 Steel Belted Radial Tires, Blackwall	N/C
QGR	P225/70R15 Steel Belted Radial Tires, White Letter	62.00
QXH	P225/60R15 Steel Belted Radial Tires, White Letter	426.00
UA1	Heavy Duty Battery	22.00
U58	AM/FM Stereo Radio	46.00
UM2	AM/FM Stereo Radio with 8-track Stereo Tape	155.00
UN3	AM/FM Stereo Radio with Stereo Cassette Tape	168.00
UP6	AM/FM Stereo Radio with CB Radio and Power Antenna	391.00
U75	Power Antenna	56.00

Factory Number	Exterior Color	Interior Color
UL5	Radio Deletion	(Credit) 126.00
U81	Dual Rear Speakers	31.00
V54	Roof Panel Carrier	135.00
YF5	California Emission Requirements	250.00
ZN1	Trailer Package	105.00

Colors

Factory Number	Exterior Color	Interior Color
19	Black	Black, Oyster, Red, Doeskin
10	White	Black, Oyster, Dark Green, Red, Dark Blue, Claret, Doeskin
13	Silver	Black, Dark Green, Red, Dark Blue, Claret, Doeskin
58	Dark Green Metallic	Oyster, Dark Green, Doeskin
83	Red	Black, Oyster, Red, Doeskin
52	Yellow	Black, Oyster
28	Dark Blue Metallic	Oyster, Dark Blue, Doeskin
59	Frost Beige	Black, Dark Green, Dark Blue, Claret
76	Dark Claret	Oyster, Claret, Doeskin
47	Dark Brown Metallic	Doeskin

1981

Identification

- [ ] Valve covers now constructed of cast magnesium.
- [ ] Newly designed closed-loop emissions control system.
- [ ] Stainless steel tubular exhaust system.
- [ ] Introduction of fiberglass-reinforced plastic single leaf rear spring.
- [ ] New six-way adjustable driver's seat.
- [ ] Standard power remote control mirrors.
- [ ] Aluminum wheels standard equipment.
- [ ] Front coil springs replaced with a fiberglass-reinforced plastic single leaf spring mounted transversely.
- [ ] Upper and lower control arms now constructed of forged aluminum.
- [ ] Optional anti-theft alarm features an ignition-interrupt system.

Specifications

Base Price: $16,258.52
Chassis and Body Numbers: St. Louis 1G1AY8764B5400001 through 5431611 Bowling Green 1G1AY8764B5100001 through 108995

I.D. Location: Left windshield pillar.
Curb Weight: 3335 lbs.
Weight Distribution: 48.2/51.8
Turning Circle: 41.3 feet
Wheelbase: 98 inches

Track, front: 58.7 inches, rear: 59.5 inches
Height: 48 inches
Length: 185.3 inches
Width: 69 inches
Steering Ratio: 17.6:1
Wheel Rim: 15 × 8
Standard Tire Size: P225/70R15

Identification Numbers

Engine Suffix: ZDD, ZDA, ZDB, ZDC,

Options

Factory No.	Item	Price
AU3	Power Door Locks, Electric	$145.00
A42	Six-way Power Seat	183.00
C49	Rear Window Defogger	119.00
CC1	Roof Panels	414.00
DG7	Twin Electric Sport Mirrors	117.00
F51	Heavy Duty Shock Absorbers, Front & Rear	37.00
FE7	Gymkhana Suspension	57.00
G92	Performance Ratio Rear Axle	20.00
K35	Cruise Control	155.00
L81	190 hp, 350 c.i. Engine	N/C
MM4	4-Speed Transmission	N/C
MX1	Turbohydramatic Transmission	N/C
NA5	Emission Equipment	N/C
N90	Aluminum Wheels	428.00
QGQ	P225/70R15 Steel Belted Radial Tires, Blackwall	N/C
QGR	P225/70R15 Steel Belted Radial Tires, White Letter	72.00
QXH	P225/60R15 Steel Belted Radial Tires, White Letter	491.92
U58	AM/FM Stereo Radio	95.00
UM4	AM/FM Stereo Radio with 8-track tape, Electronically Tuned	386.00
UM5	AM/FM Stereo Radio with CB and 8-Track Tape, Electronically Tuned	712.00
UN5	AM/FM Stereo Radio with CB and Cassette Tape, Electronically Tuned	750.00

Factory No.	Item	Price
UM6	AM/FM Stereo Radio with Cassette Tape	423.00
U75	Power Antenna	55.00
UL5	Radio Deletion	(Credit) 118.00
V54	Roof Panel Carrier	135.00
YF5	California Emission Requirements	46.00
ZN1	Trailer Package	110.00

Colors: Bowling Green, Kentucky Plant

Factory Number	Exterior Color	Interior Color
33	Silver Metallic	Silver Gray, Charcoal, Dark Red, Dark Blue
80	Claret Metallic	Silver Gray, Charcoal, Dark Red, Camel
98	Dark Claret Metallic	Silver Gray, Dark Red, Dark Blue
38	Dark Blue Metallic	Silver Gray, Camel, Dark Blue
39	Charcoal Metallic	Silver Gray, Charcoal, Dark Red
50	Beige	Charcoal, Dark Red, Camel, Dark Blue
74	Dark Bronze Metallic	Charcoal, Camel

Colors: St. Louis Plant Only

Factory Number	Exterior Color	Interior Color
10	White	Black, Doeskin, Spectra Red, Cinnabar, Dark Blue
13	Silver Metallic	Silver, Black, Spectra Red, Dark Blue
19	Black	Silver, Black, Doeskin, Spectra Red, Cinnabar
24	Bright Blue Metallic	Silver, Black, Doeskin, Dark Blue
	Dark Blue	Silver, Doeskin, Spectra Red, Dark Blue
	Frost Beige	Doeskin, Spectra Red, Cinnabar
75	Spectra Red	Silver, Black, Doeskin, Spectra Red

Factory Number	Exterior Color	Interior Color
79	Maroon Metallic	Silver, Black, Doeskin
84	Charcoal Metallic	Silver, Black, Doeskin
52	Yellow	Black

Two-Tone Combinations: Bowling Green, Kentucky Plant

Exterior Colors Upper	Lower	Interior Color
Claret Metallic	Dark Claret Metallic	Silver Gray, Dark Red, Camel
Silver Metallic	Dark Blue Metallic	Silver Gray, Dark Blue
Silver Metallic	Charcoal Metallic	Silver Gray, Charcoal, Dark Red
Beige	Dark Bronze Metallic	Camel

Stripe Identification

Color	Upper Body	Lower Body	Hood
Red	Red	Spectra Red	Dark Claret
Blue	Light Blue	Medium Blue	Dark Blue
Gray	Gray	Gray	Charcoal
Gold	Gold	Gold Wing	Dark Bronze

1982

Identification

- ☐ Throttle Body Fuel Injection replaces carburetors on all engines.
- ☐ New design camshaft features increased overlap.
- ☐ Fuelpump relocated to the interior of the fuel tank.
- ☐ Automatic four-speed transmission with overdrive feature found on all models.
- ☐ Collector Edition Corvette Hatchback Coupe offers unique features apart from the standard coupe.
- ☐ Solenoid-operated, hood-mounted fresh air inlet for engine.

Specifications

Base Price: Standard Coupe $18,765.07, Collector Edition $23,012.59
Chassis and Body Numbers: 1G1AY8786C5100001 through 5125407
I.D. Location: Left windshield pillar.
Curb Weight: 3335 lbs.
Weight Distribution: 48/52
Turning Circle: 41.3 feet
Wheelbase: 98 inches
Track, front: 58.7 inches, rear: 59.5 inches
Height: 48 inches

Length: 185.3 inches
Width: 69 inches
Steering Ratio: 17.6:1
Wheel Rim: 15 × 8
Standard Tire Size: P225/70R15

Identification Numbers

Engine Suffix: ZBA

Options

Factory No.	Item	Price
AG9	Six-way Power Seat	$199.00
AU3	Power Door Locks, Electric	$155.00
C49	Rear Window Defogger	132.00
CC1	Roof Panels	443.00
D84	Two-tone Paint	428.00
DG7	Twin Electric Sport Mirrors	125.00
FE7	Gymkhana Suspension	61.00
K35	Cruise Control	165.00
N90	Aluminum Wheels	458.00
NA5	Emission Equipment	N/C
QGQ	P225/70R15 Steel Belted Radial Tires, Blackwall	N/C
QGR	P225/70R15 Steel Belted Radial Tires, White Letter	80.00
QXH	P225/60R15 Steel Belted Radial Tires, White Letter	542.52
U58	AM/FM Stereo Radio	101.00
UM4	AM/FM Stereo Radio with 8-track tape, Electronically Tuned	386.00
UN5	AM/FM Stereo Radio with CB and Cassette Tape and Tri-band Power Antenna, Electronically Tuned	755.00
UN6	AM/FM Stereo Radio with Cassette Tape, Electronically Tuned	423.00
U75	Power Antenna	60.00
UL5	Radio Deletion	(Credit) 124.00
V54	Roof Panel Carrier	144.00
VO8	Heavy Duty Cooling	57.00
YF5	California Emission Requirements	65.00

Colors

Factory Number	Exterior Color	Interior Color
10	White	Slate, Charcoal, Carmine, Doeskin, Dark Blue, Silver, Green
13	Silver	Slate, Charcoal, Carmine, Dark Blue
19	Black	Slate, Charcoal, Carmine, Doeskin, Silver Green
24	Silver Blue Metallic	Slate, Charcoal, Dark Blue
26	Dark Blue Metallic	Slate, Doeskin, Dark Blue
31	Bright Blue Metallic	Slate, Charcoal, Doeskin, Dark Blue
39	Charcoal Metallic	Slate, Charcoal, Carmine, Doeskin
40	Silver Green Metallic	Charcoal, Silver Green
56	Gold Metallic	Charcoal, Doeskin
70	Spectra Red	Slate, Charcoal, Carmine, Doeskin
99	Dark Claret Metallic	Slate, Carmine, Doeskin

Special Edition Coupe

Exterior	Interior
Silver Beige Metallic	Silver Beige Metallic

Stripe Identification

Color	Upper Body	Lower Body	Hood
Red	Red	Spectra Red	Dark Claret Metallic
Blue	Light Blue	Medium Blue	Dark Blue Metallic
Gray	Light Gray	Gray	Charcoal

1983

There is no Corvette with the 1983 model year designation. The fourth generation Corvette, introduced in March 1983, was designated a 1984 model, and is described fully in Chapter 1.

1984

Identification

- ☐ First of the fourth-generation Corvettes.
- ☐ Full description of 1984 Corvette is found in Chapter 1.

Specifications

Base Price: $22,275.00
Chassis and Body Numbers: 1G1AY0781E5100001 up.
I.D. Location: Left front hinge pillar.
Curb Weight: 3192 lbs.
Weight Distribution: 51/49
Turning Circle: 41.4 feet
Wheelbase: 96.2 inches
Track, front: 59.6 inches, rear: 60.4 inches
Height: 46.7 inches
Length: 176.5 inches
Width: 71.0 inches
Steering Ratio: 15.5:1 std., 13.0:1 Z51 handling package
Wheel Rim: 15-7 Front, 15/7.5 Rear
Standard Tire Size: P215/65R15BW

Identification Numbers

Engine Suffix: (Not known at press time.)

Options

Factory No.	Item	Price
AG9	Power Seat, Six-way Adjustable	$210.00
AU3	Power Door Lock System	$165.00
CC3	Roof Panel	595.00
D84	Custom Two-tone	428.00
G92	Performance Ratio Axle	22.00
K34	Cruise Control	185.00
KC4	Engine Oil Cooler	158.00
L83	205 hp, 350 c.i. Engine	N/C
MM4	4-Speed transmission with Overdrive	N/C
MX0	4-Speed 700R4 Automatic Transmission With Overdrive	STD
NA5	Emission Equipment	N/C
QYZ	P215/65R15 Steel Belted Radial Tires, Blackwall	N/C
QZD	P255/50R15 Steel Belted Radial Tires, Blackwall	561.20
UM6	AM/FM Stereo Radio with Cassette Tape, Seek & Scan and Clock	153.00
UU8	Delco-GM/Bose Music System (AM/FM Stereo Radio with Cassette Tape, Seek & Scan, Clock, Special Tone and Balance controls and Four Speakers	895.00
UN8	CB Radio	215.00
UL5	Radio Deletion	(Credit) 276.00
VO1	Heavy Duty Radiator	57.00
YF5	California Emission Requirements	75.00
Z51	Performance Handling Package	600.20
Z6A	Defogger System	160.00

Colors

Exterior Color	Interior Colors
Black	Bronze, Graphite, Gray, Dark Red, Saddle
Light Blue Metallic	Blue, Graphite
Medium Blue Metallic	Blue, Graphite
Dark Bronze Metallic	Bronze
Light Bronze Metallic	Bronze

Exterior Color	*Interior Colors*
Gold Metallic	Bronze, Saddle
Gray Metallic	Graphite, Gray, Dark Red
Red	Graphite, Dark Red, Saddle
Silver Metallic	Graphite, Gray, Dark Red
White	Blue, Bronze, Graphite, Gray, Dark Red, Saddle

D84 Custom Two-Tone Paint

Exterior Color	*Accent Color*	*Interior Colors*
Light Blue Metallic	Medium Blue Metallic	Blue
Light Bronze Metallic	Dark Bronze Metallic	Bronze
Silver Metallic	Gray Metallic	Graphite, Gray, Dark Red

Chapter 3

Corvette Fuel Injection Systems

Prior to the introduction of the 1957 model year, fuel injection was not available on a mass-produced American car, either as standard equipment or as an extra-cost option. Although the technology for such a system had been available for quite some time, it required John Dolza to develop the Rochester fuel injection system into a practical and streetable state, and Zora Arkus-Duntov to apply it to the Corvette.

In its simplest description, the Rochester unit is a continuous-flow system using pressure-sensing diaphragms and mechanical linkages to measure and deliver the precise amount of fuel and airflow to each cylinder (Fig. 3-1).

The fuel injection unit employed by Chevrolet (Pontiac also used a Rochester fuel injection system) has three basic parts, along with ancillary components. These consist of the *air meter*, which supplies a vacuum control signal to the fuel meter in response to engine load; the *fuel meter*, whch interprets that vacuum control signal and regulates fuel flow to the injector nozzles; and the *intake manifold*, commonly called a *plenum*, which provides a distribution system for the rammed air flow to the cylinders.

OPERATION
Air Meter

The air meter consists of three basic parts: the *throttle valve*, the *cold enrichment valve*, and the *air meter body* (Fig. 3-2).

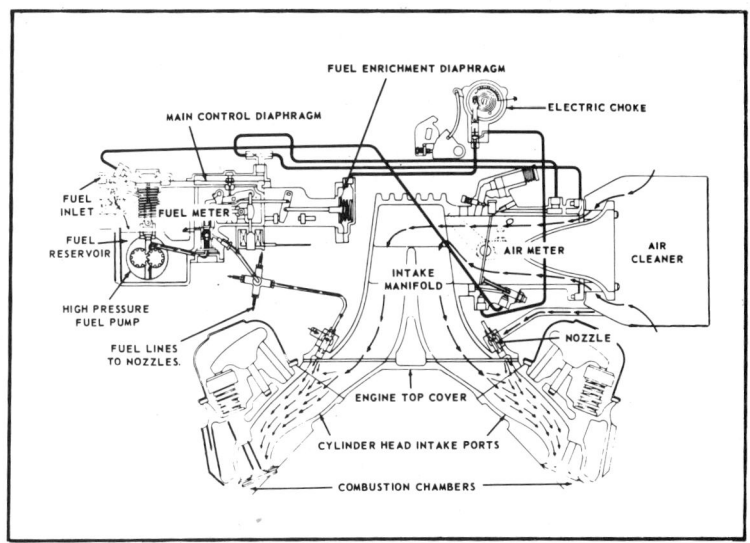

Fig. 3-1. John Dolza and Zora Arkus-Duntov created and refined the Rochester Ramjet fuel injection system. First offered in 1957, the popular option was available from 1957 through 1965.

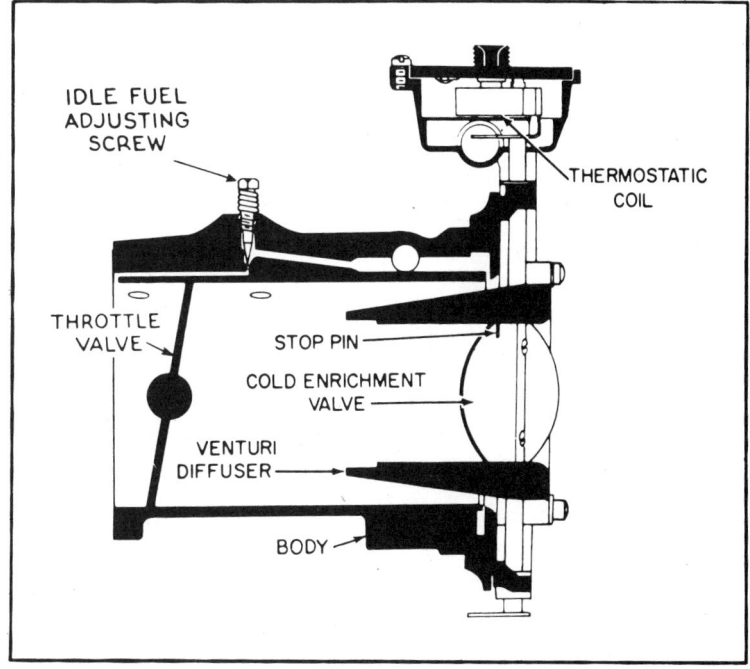

Fig. 3-2. Air meter.

The function of the throttle valve is to control the air as it passes into the system. It is connected mechanically to the accelerator pedal.

The diffuser cone is suspended in the bore of the air meter inlet. Its design provides a highly efficient annular venturi between the air meter and the cone. This venturi design provides the minimum air flow restriction, which is a vital factor in engine breathing capabilities.

Housed in the air meter body are the following components, plus the idle and main venturi signal systems.

Main Venturi Signal

The main venturi signals are generated at the venturi as the air flows past an annular opening formed between the air meter body and the machined piezometer ring (Fig. 3-3).

This venturi vacuum signal will always be a direct measure of air flowing to the engine; as a consequence, the signal can be used to automatically control fuel air ratios to the engine.

Idle Air

Up to 40 percent of the air requirements of the engine at idle enter by way of the nozzle blocks from an air connection tapped into the air meter body. The remaining air is controlled by adjusting the throttle valve position with the positive idle stop screw found on the air meter. Turning the screw in increases idle speed, while turning the screw out decreases the idle.

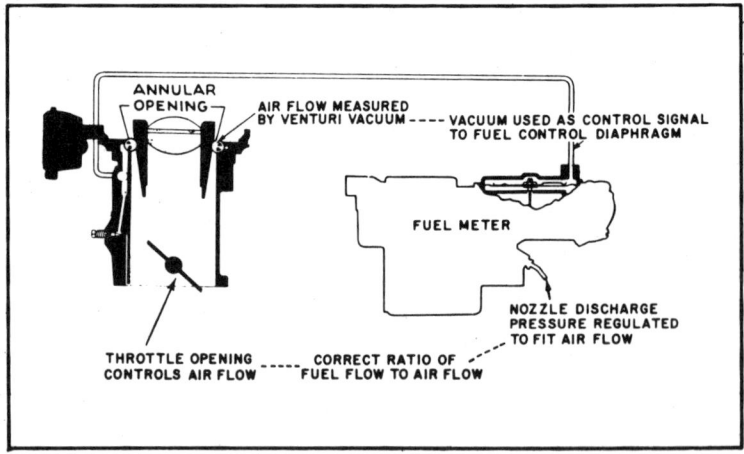

Fig. 3-3. Main control signal.

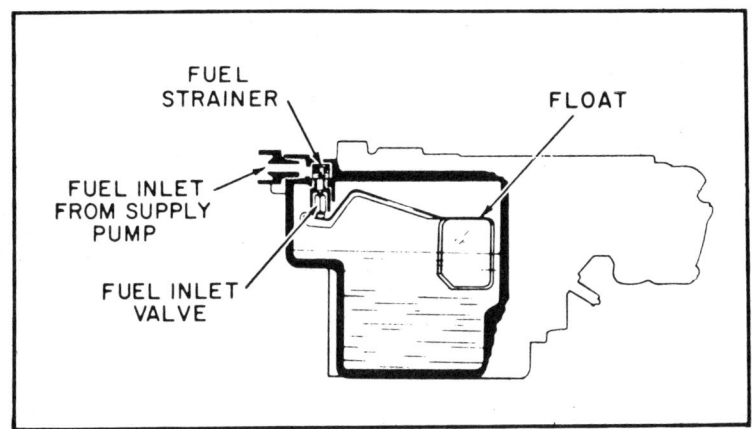

Fig. 3-4. Fuel meter.

Fuel Meter

The fuel meter contains a fuel reservoir controlled by a float very similar to that used in a conventional carburetor. Fuel is supplied to the fuel meter by the engine fuel pump. Fuel enters the system through a 10-micron filter, passes through the fuel inlet valve, and empties directly into the main reservoir where it is picked up by a high pressure gear pump (Fig. 3-4).

High Pressure Wobble Pump

The precise, high pressure wobble pump is located in the lower part of the fuel meter reservoir and is normally completely submerged at all times. The pump is driven by a flexible shaft deriving its power from the distributor. It rotates at half the engine speed. Fuel pressure varies from about zero to approximately 200 psi, depending upon engine speed. Fuel not used by the injection system is routed back to the fuel meter by means of a fuel control system.

Fuel Control System

Fuel flow from the high pressure wobble pump must be regulated to provide correct flow to the nozzles. The new design, 1963-65 model, is designed with a recirculating fuel flow system from the high pressure pump to the nozzle distributor and back to the fuel meter spill ports. The control of fuel flow in the Rochester system is regulated by the amount of fuel spilled or bypassed away from the nozzle circuits. A three-piece valve is located parallel to the nozzles on the pressure side of the pump. When high fuel flow is required, the spill valve is moved downward, closing off the spill ports to the fuel meter reservoir. This prevents the fuel from bypassing the nozzle circuits and increases fuel flow to the nozzles. Conversely, the spill valve must be raised to allow the spill ports to be exposed when low fuel flow is required. This action causes the main output of the pump to bypass the nozzle circuits and re-enter the meter reservoir through the spill ports (Fig. 3-5).

The accelerator pedal is not directly connected to the spill plunger. Fuel control is accomplished by a very precise mechanical linkage control system. This linkage system is carefully counterbalanced so that the only forces influencing the system are fuel pressure and diaphragm pressure. This precise balancing of the linkage makes the unit extremely sensitive to slight changes in venturi vacuum signal on the main control diaphragm.

The ratio of diaphragm vacuum to fuel pressure and the corresponding fuel/air ratio is controlled by the location of the control lever pivot point in the fuel meter. Moving the ratio lever changes the mechanical advantages of the linkage system, thus providing fuel/air ratios for all driving ranges. For normal driving (engine manifold vacuum above 8 inches of mercury), the ratio is held at the "economy" stop and fuel flow is a result of main control diaphragm vacuum. When increased performance is desired, the ratio lever is

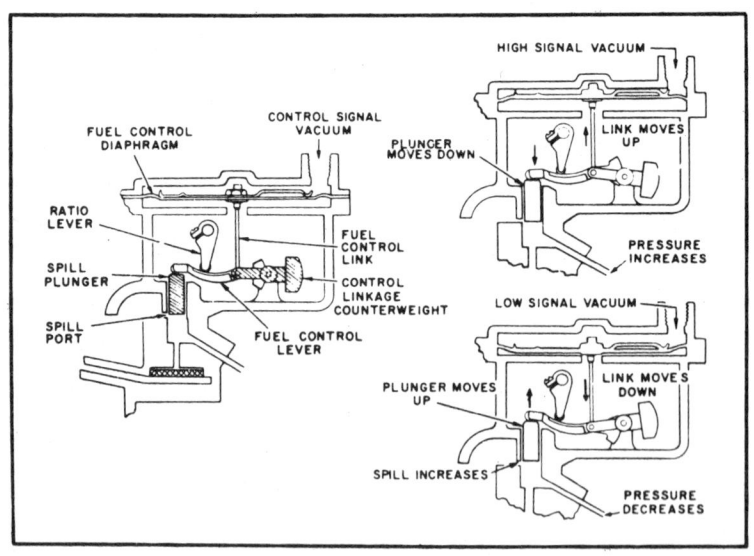

Fig. 3-5. Fuel control linkage.

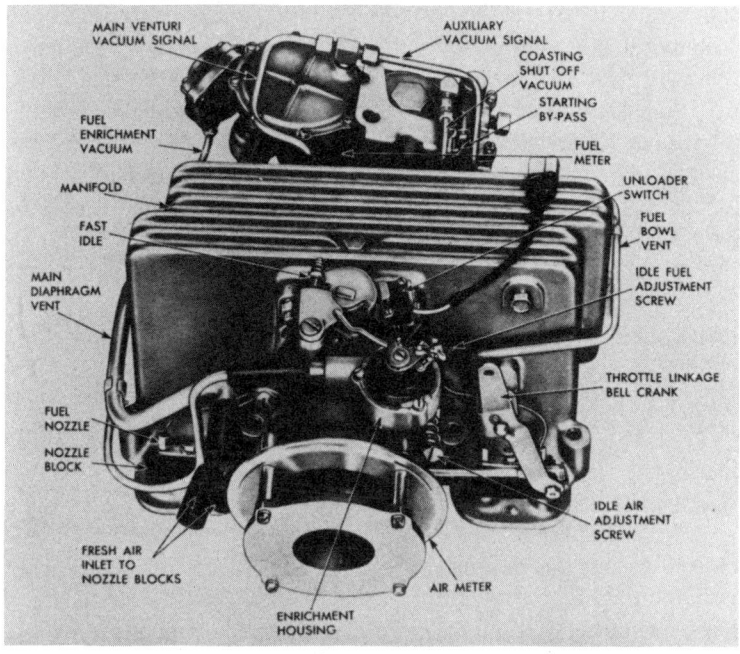

Fig. 3-6. Although operation and maintenance of the fuel injection system appears complicated, once set up properly, it will perform well and offer trouble-free operation.

moved to the "power" stop. This action increases the mechanical advantage during engine power demands, closes the spill ports, and increases fuel to the nozzles (Fig. 3-6).

Operation of the fuel injection system is fairly straightforward and essentially troublefree. Once properly set up by a knowledgeable technician, the system requires no more attention than a carbureted engine. The operating principles consist of the following:

Starting System

Cold engine starting conditions require that extra fuel be introduced to compensate for poor fuel evaporation. Unlike a carbureted engine, pumping the accelerator pedal will not provide this fuel since there is no accelerator pump. The accelerator should be depressed once and then released, allowing the throttle to be preset for starting by the fast idle cam. During cranking, the signal generated at the idle needle and air meter venturi is very low and has to be boosted. This boost comes from a spring-loaded open cranking signal valve located at the enrichment diaphragm housing. The open cranking signal value allows direct manifold cranking vacuum to react on and lift the main control diaphragm, closing the spill valve. Additionally, the enrichment diaphragm is spring-loaded to hold the ratio lever at the "power" stop, thus maximum fuel flow is available at cranking. Immediately after starting, or when manifold vacuum reaches 1 inch of mercury, the engine manifold vacuum overcomes the springs in the cranking signal valve and enrichment diaphragm, and the fuel injection system operates on the normal idle circuit.

Idle Circuit

To achieve the maximum signal at the control diaphragm during cold engine idle, several operations take place.

1. The fast idle cam holds the throttle valve open slightly, increasing the velocity of air flow through the venturi, which increases the venturi vacuum signal to the main control diaphragm.

2. The thermostatically controlled choke valve is also held closed during the initial cold engine operation, forcing a higher percentage of air to pass through the venturi. This allows the use of a discernible venturi signal even at relatively low engine speeds.

3. The enrichment diaphragm is connected directly to the manifold vacuum and this moves the ratio lever to the "economy" stop as soon as manifold vacuum overcomes the diaphragm spring. As the warmed air relaxes the thermostat, thus allowing the choke valve to open, less air flows through the venturi and the signal generated here drops. At this point, the idle signal system then becomes the more important signal.

Fuel control during engine warmup is accomplished through the idle circuit acting on the main control diaphragm. With the ratio lever at the "economy" stop, air for combustion now enters as previously described through the idle air circuit and the vented nozzle blocks.

Hot Idle Compensator

During extreme heat conditions, vaporizing fuel can cause rich idling, which results in engine roughness and stalling.

A thermostatically operated valve is located on the top of the air meter throttle valve and this valve opens, exposing a calibrated orifice through the throttle valve. This valve opens as temperatures increase, allowing a predetermined amount of air to bleed into the over-rich manifold and restore the idle mixture to its correct value.

The compensator is factory-calibrated and no adjustment is necessary; however, it should be replaced if defective.

Acceleration

During normal driving speeds, acceleration is instantaneous. As the throttle is opened, three operations take place to provide the correct amount of fuel.

1. Opening of the throttle valve causes an increase in air flow, which increases the venturi signal at the main diaphragm.

2. This momentary reduction of manifold vaccum causes the ratio lever to move to the power stop.

3. The calibrated restriction in the main control signal circuit retains any signal left prior to the accelerator demands, thus adding to the total signal before it bleeds through the restriction.

Power

The air/fuel mixtures required during power demands are very similar to those required during acceleration. The wide-open throttle causes a reduction in manifold vacuum and the ratio lever moves to the "power" stop. What becomes more important, however, is the radically increased air flow and corresponding venturi signal directed to the main diaphragm.

Hot Starting and Unloading

Hot starting and unloading operations, obviously, do not require additional fuel. For hot starting, the throttle valve should be held one quarter to one half open to prevent high manifold vacuum at the cranking signal valve. In the event of a flooded engine, the throttle valve should be held wide open during cranking. With the increased volume of air and a reduced flow of fuel, the engine should start.

Servicing of the Rochester injection system falls into two distinct categories, routine maintenance and detailed service operations, both of which can be undertaken by the adept shade-tree mechanic.

ROUTINE MAINTENANCE AND ADJUSTMENTS
Fuel Filter

The fuel filter is of the non-serviceable type and cannot be cleaned and reused. It should be replaced every 15,000 miles.

Replacement of the filter involves disconnecting the fuel lines to the filter and removing it from its mounting bracket.

Air Cleaner

The air cleaner is of the serviceable type and can be cleaned and reused. It is constructed of polyurethane and the element should be cleaned every 8,000 miles. Servicing consists of the following steps:

1. Loosen the flexible hose clamp on the air meter adaptor and cover clamps at the air cleaner. Remove the hose and air cleaner cover from the engine.

2. Remove the washable element from the air cleaner housing and the inner support.

3. Wash the element thoroughly in solvent and squeeze the excess solvent from it. Rinse in light oil, again squeezing all of the excess liquid from the element. Install the element in the air cleaner housing and reverse the removal procedure.

Note: Never shake or swing the element. This may cause the polyurethane to tear. Instead, gently squeeze the material until the excess is removed.

Idle Speed and Fuel

Note: All on-vehicle adjustments should be made with the engine at full operating temperature.

1. Preset the idle mixture screw 1½ turns out from the fully closed position.

Fig. 3-7. Adjusting idle mixture screw.

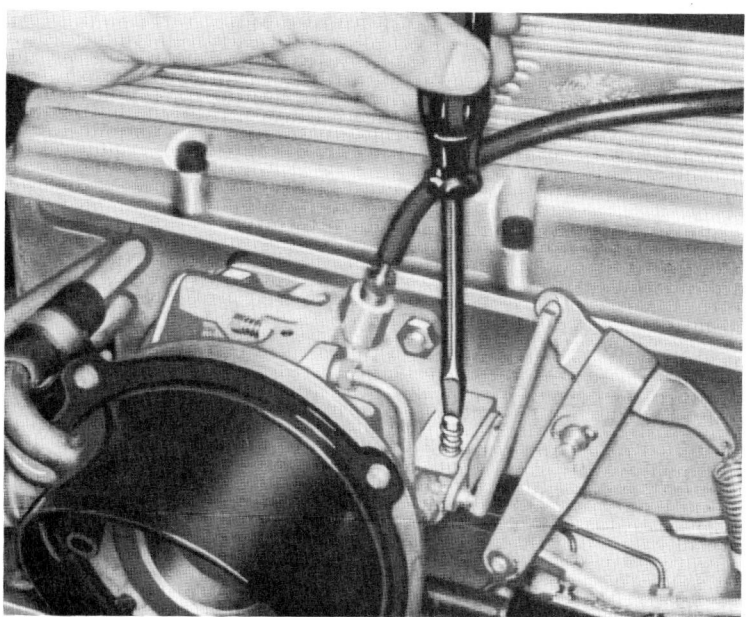

Fig. 3-8. Adjusting idle speed screw.

2. With the engine at operating temperature and running, bring the idle speed up to the appropriate specifications by adjusting the idle speed screw.

3. At this point, the idle mixture screw may be adjusted to obtain the best engine idle characteristics. By adjusting this screw, the idle speed screw may have to be readjusted to obtain the desired 800-850 rpm (Fig. 3-8).

Fast Idle

1. Check the fast idle cam and the adjusting screw for the proper off position clearance. Bend the linkage to obtain the clearance desired (Fig. 3-9).

2. With the engine off, crack the throttle valve and position the cold enrichment valve to its closed position. Release the throttle linkage, noting that the fast idle cam will now be positioned in the cold engine operation position. Release the cold enrichment valve, restart the engine, and adjust the fast idle screw to obtain 2200 rpm.

Cold Enrichment

The only cold enrichment adjustment required is to set the cold enrichment cover to three notches lean.

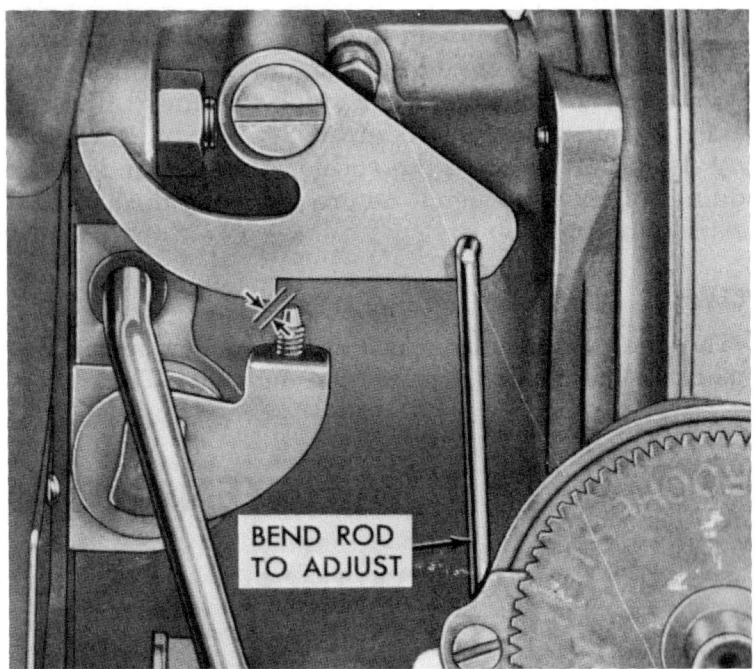

Fig. 3-9. Fast idle linkage clearance.

Ratio Lever Stop Settings

The following information requires the use of Chevrolet special tool J-7090, manometer.

Manometer Installation

1. Attach the manometer in a convenient location in the engine compartment. Use the two-position bracket to obtain the most vertical position possible.

2. Level the unit using the leveling vial.

3. Open both water manometer valves and check the water manometer to see if a zero reading can be obtained. Adjust to zero by means of the oil leveling screw.

Note: Add red oil, with a specific gravity of 0.826, if a zero reading cannot be obtained. Back the leveling screw out for this procedure.

4. Remove both hose adapters on the mercury (Hg) side of the manometer and knock out the plug in each adapter.

5. Install the T adapter into the most easily accessible point in the fuel nozzle circuit (Fig. 3-10).

6. Connect fuel pressure line to the T fitting and the Mercury side of the manometer. Be certain that the fuel trap inlet is located properly in line.

7. Connect the venturi signal line with clamp to the cranking signal valve line and the water side of the manometer.

Note: Be certain the clamp is secure; otherwise, the high vacuum generated will cause the red oil to be lost.

8. Remove the main diaphragm vent tube and install the larger rubber tube in its place.

9. Set up the mercury manometer at zero inches by sliding the scale up or down. Check the leveling vial and adjust as necessary. Manometer unit is now ready for economy stop settings.

Economy Stop Settings

1. Bring engine to operating temperature. Check to see if the fuel injection unit is operating on the economy stop setting.

Note: Some units will start hard with the cranking signal valve disconnected. It may be necessary to reconnect this line during the initial starting procedure.

2. Bring up the engine rpm until a 0.5 inch signal is observed on the water manometer. It may be necessary to engage the fast idle cam to achieve this setting. Take a reading on the mercury manometer. Return the engine to idle and repeat the procedure. Record the readings from at least three trials and average the

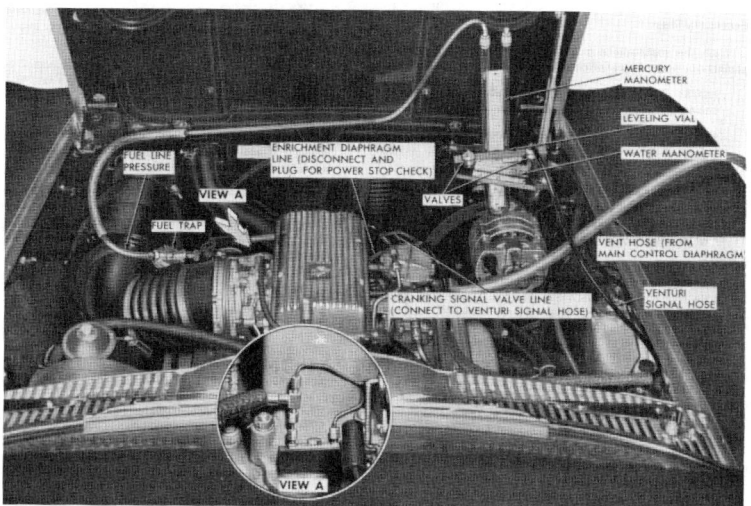

Fig. 3-10. Manometer installation (typical).

Table 3-1. Fuel Injection Specifications.

Power Stop @ .5" H$_2$O	1.2 (± .1 Hg.)
Economy Stop @ .5" H$_2$O	.8 (± .1 Hg.)
Fast Idle Speed (rpm-hot engine)	2000
Enrichment Diaphragm Clearance (Min.)	.040"
Cold Enrichment Housing Cover Index	Index
Cranking Signal Valve-Vacuum to Apply (" Hg. Max.)	1"
Enrichment Diaphragm-Vacuum to Apply (" Hg.)	Economy Stop — 9"
	Power Stop — 3"
Main Signal Diaphragm-Vacuum to Apply (" H$_2$O)	½" to 30" H$_2$O
Float Level	2 9/32
Float Drop	2 27/32

results. See specifications, Table 3-1. This completes the steps for the economy stop reading (Fig. 3-11).

Power Stop Settings

1. Maintain the manometer hookup as in the economy stop readings.

Fig. 3-11. Ratio lever stop locations.

2. In addition, disconnect and plug the vacuum line going to the enrichment diaphragm. This causes the fuel injection unit to operate only on the power stop.

Note: This practice will cause spark plug fouling if done for a prolonged period of time. Take appropriate steps if this condition occurs.

3. Bring up the engine rpm until a 0.5 inch signal is observed on the water manometer. Also take a reading on the mercury manometer. Lower the engine speed and repeat the procedure at least three times, recording the readings and averaging the results. See specifications, Table 3-1. This completes the steps for the power stop reading.

Note: Be certain that the enrichment diaphragm is not bottoming in the housing.

SERVICE OPERATIONS
Injection Assembly Removal

1. Disconnect washer vacuum line at its manifold fitting, accelerator linkage at the throttle bellcrank, choke heat tubes, and bellcrank return spring.

2. Loosen the clamp that retains the flexible hose to the air meter and the clamps at the air cleaner cover. Slide the hose from the air meter adapter. Remove the hose and air cleaner assembly.

3. Disconnect the fuel line at the fuel meter and positive crankcase ventilation hoses at the valve and oil filler tube. Disconnect distributor spark advance hose at the air meter.

4. Disconnect the drive cable coupling at the distributor and slide the cable into the pump housing to disengage it from the distributor. Pull the cable clear of the distributor and remove it from engine compartment.

5. Remove the manifold-to-engine adapter plate retaining nuts and carefully remove the fuel injection unit.

Note: During bench procedures, it is advisable to install a ⅜" × 2" bolt and nut in each manifold mounting hole to prevent damage to the nozzle assemblies.

Injector Assembly Installation

Chevrolet recommends that when a complete overhaul involving nozzle cleaning is made, the fuel nozzle spray pattern check be made. Use a suitable drive mechanism (such as an air wrench or electric drill) to operate the gear pump while oral vacuum is applied to the main control diaphragm. The vacuum assures that all fuel will

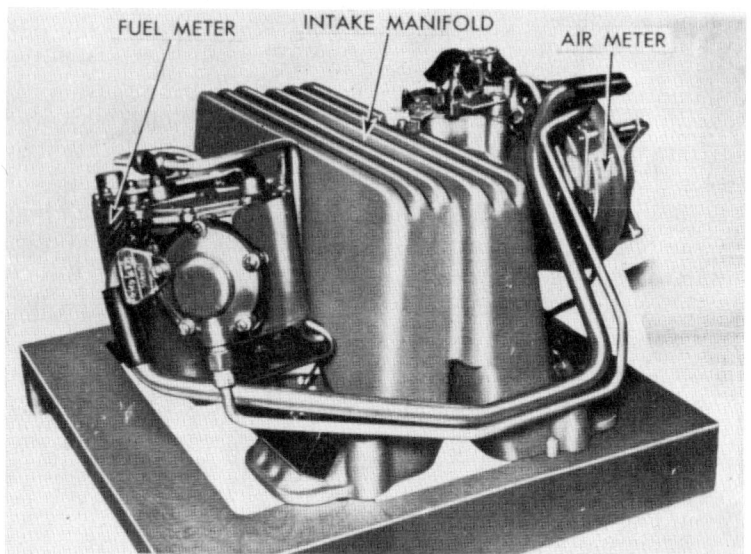

Fig. 3-12. The spray pattern for injectors can be checked by placing the fuel injection unit on a bench and operating the gear pump with an electric drill.

pass into the nozzle circuit. The spray pattern should be such that each bank of nozzles appear as a single spray when viewed from the end of the injector unit (Fig. 3-12).

1. Remove the bench disassembly feet and carefully place the injection assembly on the engine adapter plate. Install nuts and torque to 15-20 foot-pounds.

2. Install the fuel meter pump drive cable and housing. Slide the cable and the housing into the gear pump first, align the cable with the distributor drive gear, and connect the cable housing to the distributor.

Note: Be certain that the fiber washer is correctly placed at the distributor end of the drive cable.

3. Connect the fuel line to the fuel meter.

4. Connect the choke heat tube at choke housing and the spark advance hose to the air meter.

5. Connect clean air tube, main diaphragm, vent tube, and crankcase ventilation hoses at the air cleaner hose adapter.

6. Install air cleaner cover and flex hose.

7. Connect accelerator rod and return spring and adjust.

8. Adjust the speed, mixture, and ratio lever stops as outlined previously.

Air Meter Removal

1. Disconnect the throttle return spring and the accelerator linkage at the throttle bellcrank. Remove the bellcrank retaining clip and slide it from the pivot shaft, leaving it attached to the shaft.
2. Remove air cleaner cover and flexible hose. Disconnect the main control diaphragm vent tube and positive ventilation tube at adapter.
3. Disconnect choke clean air tubes at adapter and choke housing.
4. Disconnect the main control signal tube at both ends and lower it out of the way. Disconnect spark advance hose at the air meter.
5. Remove the four air meter-to-manifold retaining nuts. Remove the air meter from unit while simultaneously disconnecting the rubber nozzle balance tube elbow at the air meter.

Air Meter Disassembly

1. Remove the four screws holding the air cleaner adapter to

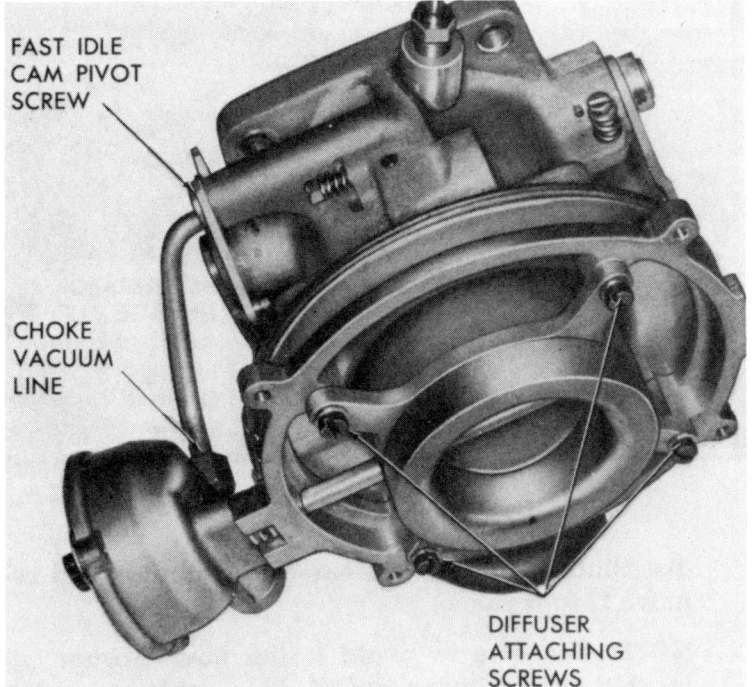

Fig. 3-13. Removing diffuser assembly.

the air meter and remove it.

2. Remove the four diffuser assembly screws; remove the fast idle cam pivot screw; remove the diffuser choke assembly and the piezometer ring from the air meter (Fig. 3-13).

3. Remove the idle speed and the idle fuel adjusting screws.

4. It is not necessary to remove the throttle or choke valve unless shaft binding is occurring.

Note: Do not clean air meter restrictions by passing wire through the orifices. Use only solvent and air for this procedure. Also, do not wipe the bores of the air meter with a cloth.

Choke Valve Assembly

The choke coil and cover assembly is held in place with three retaining screws. To replace the unit, simply remove the screws and disconnect the heat tube. The new cover should be indexed to the housing when installed.

Complete disassembly of the choke valve is as follows:

1. Remove the four screws retaining the choke and diffuser assembly to the air meter. Disconnect the vacuum heat tube and remove the fast idle cam pivot screw. Remove the choke and diffuser assembly from the air meter.

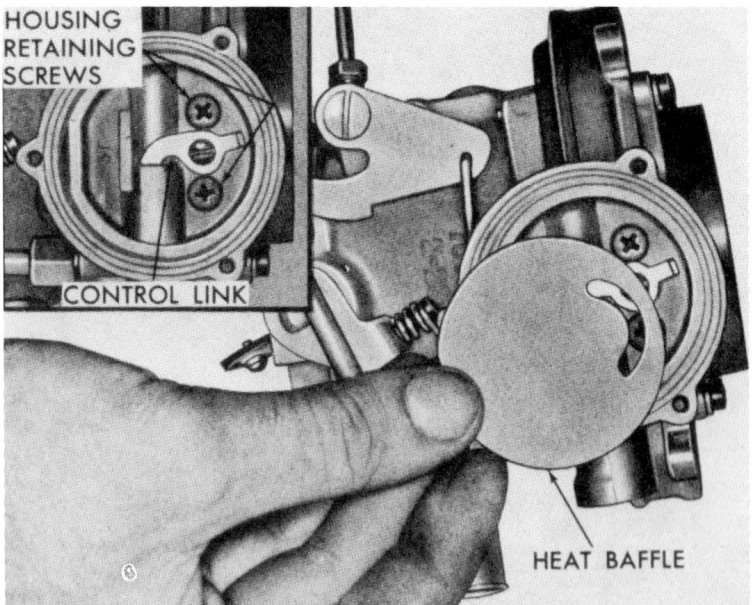

Fig. 3-14. Choke heat baffle and control link.

2. Remove the coil and cover as detailed above. Remove the heat baffle and control link. Remove the two choke housing screws along with the choke housing (Fig. 3-14).

3. Remove the choke valve from the shaft and slide the shaft from the housing. The choke linkage may remain on the shaft.

4. To reassemble, reverse the procedures. Check to see that the choke action is working properly.

Throttle Valve Removal

Servicing the throttle valve consists mainly of eliminating conditions that cause binding of the shaft. Prior to disassembly, first soak the throttle valve unit in solvent. If this does not correct the binding, proceed with the following steps:

1. Remove the roll pin retaining the throttle linkage to the shaft linkage.

2. Remove the throttle valve retaining screws and file the burrs from the throttle shaft.

3. Remove the throttle valve from the shaft and remove the shaft from the air meter housing.

4. Clean the shaft and air meter bushings and reassemble. Check to see that the shaft rotates freely in the air meter before reassembly.

5. To reassemble, reverse the above procedures.

Air Meter Assembly

1. Install the throttle valve assembly.

2. Install idle speed and idle fuel adjusting screws. Set each screw 1½ turns out from the bottom.

Note: Replace the idle fuel screw if the valve end appears damaged.

3. Position the gasket, piezometer ring, and diffuser assembly on the air meter and install. Install the fast idle cam pivot screw and linkage (Fig. 3-15).

Note: Piezometer ring and air cleaner may be installed without reference to original installation.

4. Attach the air cleaner flexible hose adapter to the air meter.

Air Meter Installation

1. Install the air meter assembly to manifold while carefully aligning rubber elbow at the nozzle vent tube. Install retaining nuts and lockwashers.

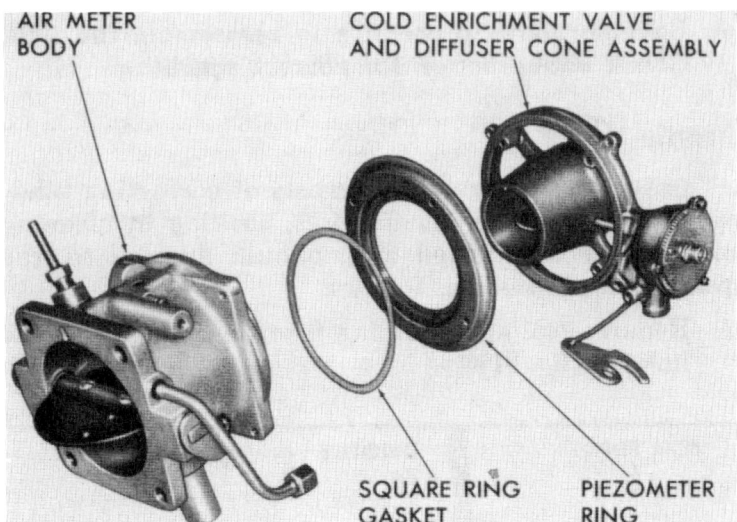

Fig. 3-15. Air meter assembly.

2. Connect the main signal tube at both ends by starting with the air meter end first.

3. Position the throttle bellcrank on the pivot shaft and retain with clip. Install the return spring and linkage.

4. Install the choke heat tube, clean air tube, main diaphragm vent tube, and crankcase ventilation tube.

5. Install air cleaner cover and hose assembly.

Note: Peen the throttle and choke valve screw ends at time of reassembly to prevent them from falling out.

Fuel Meter Removal

1. Remove the main control signal tube from unit.

2. Disconnect the main diaphragm vent tube and cranking signal vacuum line at the fuel meter.

3. Disconnect the enrichment diaphragm tube at both ends; remove the manifold end first.

4. Invert unit and drain fuel bowl through cover vent.

5. Invert unit and disconnect fuel pressure lines at each nozzle and at the central "spyder."

Note: These lines must be removed carefully to avoid damage.

6. Remove the lower mounting bracket-to-meter screws and upper bracket-to-manifold screw and lift from meter.

7. Reverse the removal to install new O-rings at fuel line connection.

Note: Install the O-rings dry to prevent the rings from rolling over the shoulder of the nozzle distribution line.

Fuel Meter Cleaning and Inspection

Wash all of the metal parts in clean solvent and dry with compressed air. Do not wash rubber parts or diaphragms. Replace these items when they show aging or stiffness. The main control diaphragm should appear very supple; replace if necessary.

Nozzle cleaning can be accomplished by following the procedures outlined previously.

Inspect all castings for cracks, plugged tubes, and passages. Check carefully the main control diaphragm linkage, castings, and axle shafts for cracks and wear. Check valve mechanisms for wear or binding.

Check the integral siphon breaker ball for movement. If frozen, soak in solvent.

Check the cranking signal valve by applying not more than 1 inch of Hg vacuum. In most cases, oral vacuum will be sufficient to determine a leaking diaphragm.

Fuel Meter Disassembly & Assembly

The cranking signal valve is nonserviceable and is simply replaced if found defective. Simply disconnect the vacuum line and replace the valve.

Enrichment Diaphragm

1. Remove the ratio lever shield retaining screws and remove shield.
2. Remove vacuum lines from the manifold and the cranking signal valve.
3. Remove the clip retaining shaft to ratio lever and the two diaphragm housing screws; remove enrichment diaphragm assembly.
4. Disassemble the housing and replace the diaphragm.

Note: Center the diaphragm in housing before tightening the cover.

5. Reinstall the assembly to the fuel meter housing.
6. Check the clearance between housing and diaphragm. This should be a minimum of .040" to prevent interference during the Power Stop operation. Change the diaphragm length to correct the clearance being careful to hold the shaft while loosening the lock nut.

Note: Correct positioning of the enrichment diaphragm may be checked by applying a vacuum source to the cover fitting. The ratio lever should leave the Power Stop at 4 inches of vacuum for altitudes below 6000 feet and at 2 inches at altitudes above 6000 feet.

Main Control Diaphragm

1. Disconnect vacuum lines at the diaphragm cover T fitting.
2. Remove the retaining screws and separate the cover from the diaphragm.
3. Check diaphragm for tears, ruptures, wrinkles, aging, and free fall to confirm diagnosis.
4. Remove the nut retaining the diaphragm to control link and remove the diaphragm (Fig. 3-16).

Note: The control link must be held from rotating to prevent damage to the linkage.

5. Install the new diaphragm and gasket on the link and tighten the retaining link.

Caution: The slots in the diaphragm should align naturally with the cover attaching holes located in the bowl cover. Repeat the above steps until this condition is present. Do not try to force the diaphragm holes to line up with the attaching screw holes. Occasionally some diaphragms appear to be very tight; this is a defective

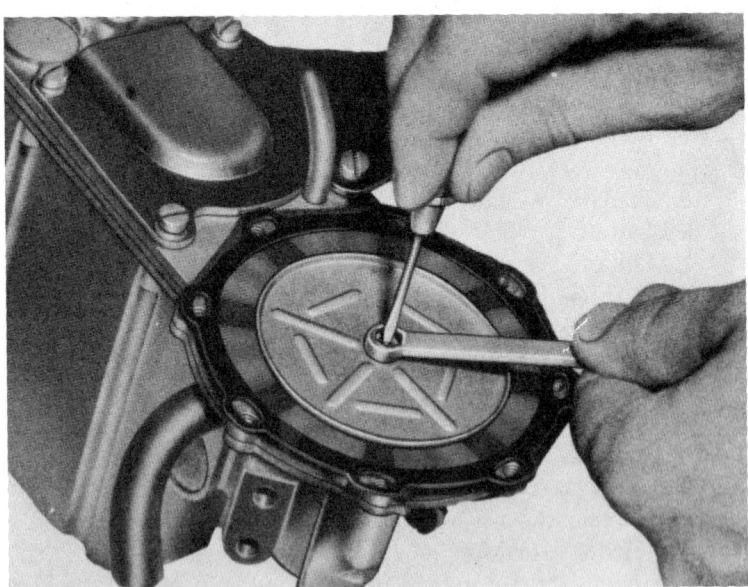

Fig. 3-16. Removing main diaphragm retaining nut.

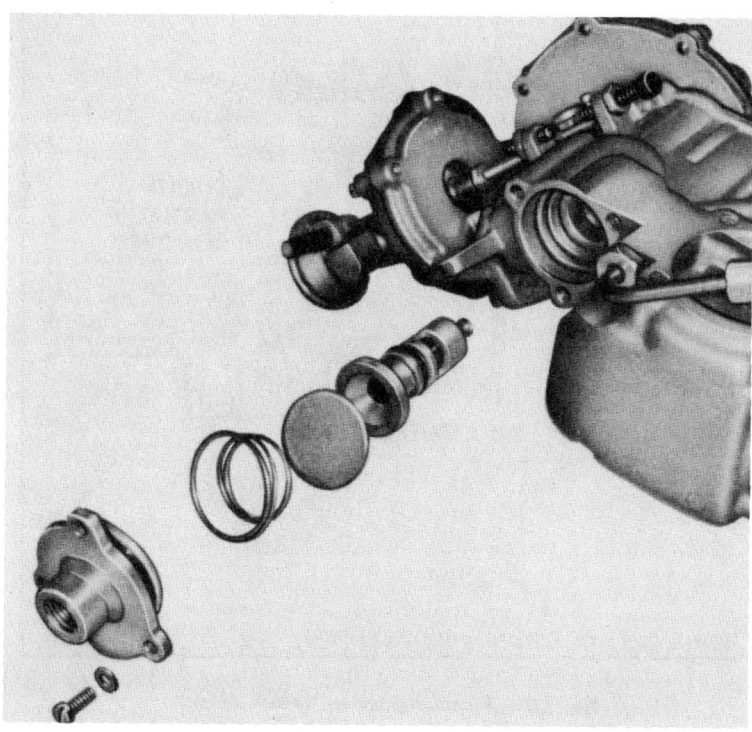

Fig. 3-17. Spill valve assembly.

diaphragm. Be careful not to duplicate this condition when installing the new diaphragm.

Note: Calibration of the fuel injection unit will not be affected by replacement of the diaphragm.

Spill Valve Assembly (Off Vehicle)

1. Disconnect the fuel line at the spill valve cover.
2. Remove the three cover retaining screws and remove cover, spring, and fuel filter screen.
3. Remove the spill valve and sleeve assembly.

Note: Use a hook-shaped device of heavy wire engaged in the lower spill holes of the sleeve.

4. Using gasoline as a lubricant, check the valve action for sticking or sluggish action. Replace or clean the valve and sleeve when necessary.
5. Installation is the reverse of steps 1 through 3 (Fig. 3-17).

155

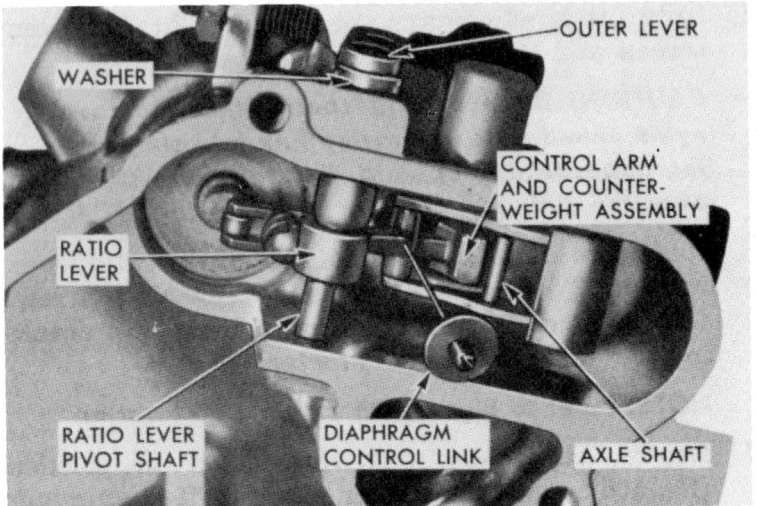

Fig. 3-18. Control linkage location.

Control Arm and Counterweight Assembly

1. Remove the main control diaphragm as detailed above.
2. Remove the nylon shield at the diaphragm control link and the nine fuel bowl attaching screws. Lift the bowl cover, upper support bracket, vent screen, and gasket from the meter body (Fig. 3-18).

Caution: Do not bend the control link. Remove the nylon shield by first starting the link into the slot and then prying the opposite side upward. Turn shield over the link to finish removal.

3. Remove the enrichment control rod clip at the ratio lever, remove the two enrichment housing attaching screws, remove the enrichment housing and crankcase signal valve from the meter.
4. Loosen the screw retaining the ratio lever in position. Slide the ratio lever pivot shaft from the meter body and remove the ratio lever (Fig. 3-19).
5. Remove the control arm and counterweights on axle until the axle shaft is exposed. Press the axle from the meter housing using long-nosed pliers. Remove the control arm and counterweight assembly from the fuel meter (Fig. 3-20).

Note: This procedure will also remove the lead sealing ball located on the outer end of the axle shaft.

6. Position the control arm and counterweight assembly in the fuel meter and install the axle shaft and lead sealing ball.

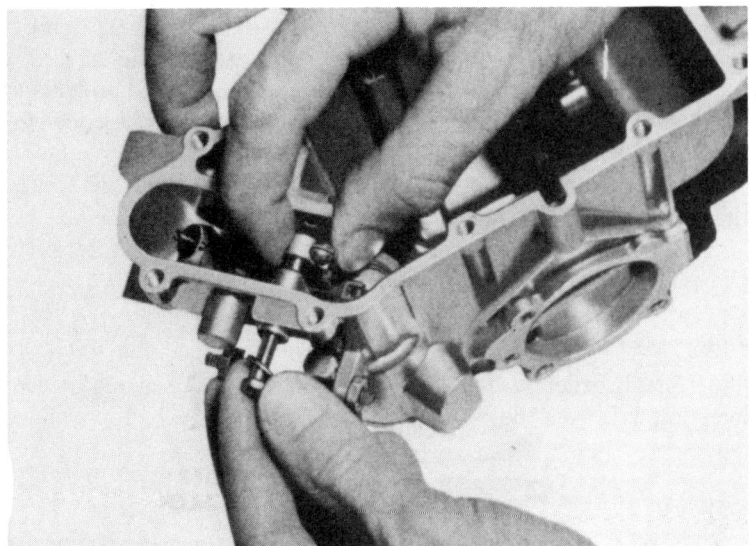

Fig. 3-19. Removing ratio lever from meter.

7. Position the ratio lever in the fuel meter, install the ratio lever shaft, and tighten the retaining screw securely.

8. Before positioning the fuel meter body, check the fuel reservoir float settings. Float level should be 2 9/32 inches, while float drop should be 2 27/32 inches. Bend the float drop or the tang to make the proper adjustments.

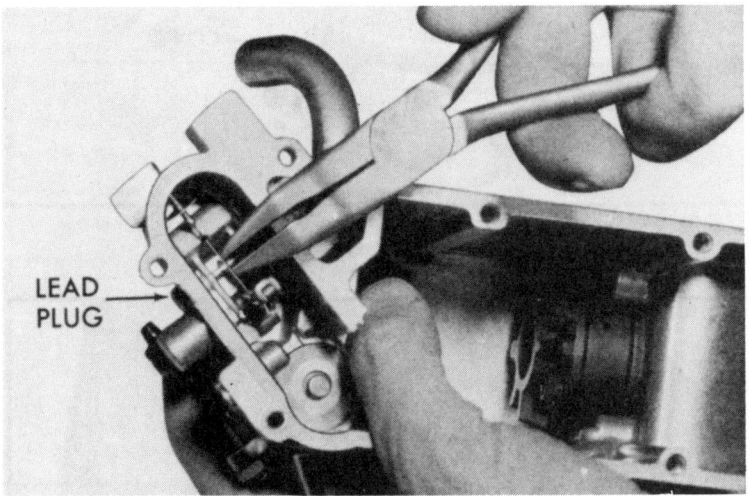

Fig. 3-20. Removing control arm axle shaft.

9. Position the fuel bowl gasket, cover, and upper support bracket on the fuel meter and secure with the attaching screws.

Caution: Be certain that the diaphragm control link protrudes through the cover hole before attaching and securing the cover to the meter.

10. Install the nylon shield at the diaphragm control link. Start the link into the shield slot and work the shield into position.

11. Install the main control diaphragm and cover as detailed above.

High Pressure Pump Disassembly & Assembly

Note: In order to avoid gas spillage onto the engine, remove the injection unit from the vehicle before removing the high-pressure pump.

Removal

1. Remove the fuel meter assembly from the manifold.
2. Remove the five access screws that attach the fuel meter. Remove the pump and gasket from the meter (Fig. 3-21).

High Pressure Disassembly

Note: A seal kit is available for servicing; however, other damaged parts may require that the pump be replaced. Disassemble in a large box in order that the small parts will not become lost. There are 48 pieces plus screws.

1. Remove the two discharge housing retaining screws and

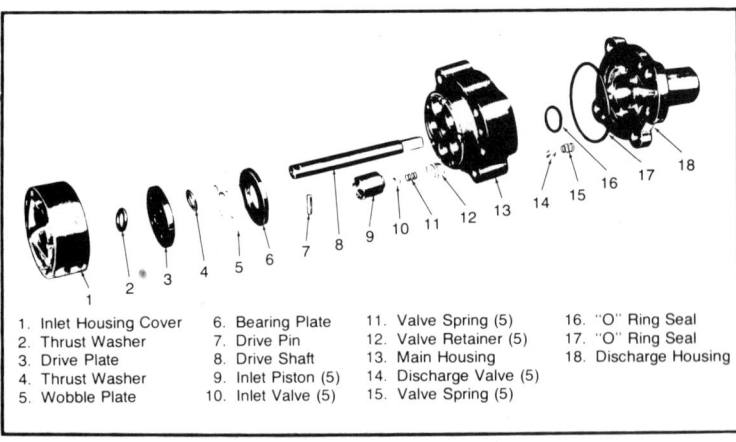

1. Inlet Housing Cover
2. Thrust Washer
3. Drive Plate
4. Thrust Washer
5. Wobble Plate
6. Bearing Plate
7. Drive Pin
8. Drive Shaft
9. Inlet Piston (5)
10. Inlet Valve (5)
11. Valve Spring (5)
12. Valve Retainer (5)
13. Main Housing
14. Discharge Valve (5)
15. Valve Spring (5)
16. "O" Ring Seal
17. "O" Ring Seal
18. Discharge Housing

Fig. 3-21. Fuel pump exploded view.

remove the housing. Now remove the five discharge valves and springs.

2. Hold unit with inlet cover upright and remove the five cover retaining screws.

3. Remove the cover and pull drive shaft up and out of the pump by holding the wobble plate.

Note: Mark the pistons for easier reassembly.

4. Remove the five pump pistons and their inlet valve assemblies.

5. Inspect all parts for wear and damage. The pistons must operate freely in their cylinders. Also, check for wear or breakage on the wobble plate and associated parts.

6. Remove the seal rings from the pump housing and discharge housing.

7. If warranted, measure the location of the drive shaft seal and then press it from the discharge housing using a suitable driver.

8. With a good sealing compound, coat the outer diameter of the shaft seal. Press seal into housing to same location as measured previously.

High-Pressure Pump Assembly

1. Assemble the inlet valve springs, valve assembly, pistons and pistons springs into the housing (Fig. 3-22).

2. Assemble the drive shaft and wobble plate.

3. Install the drive shaft and the wobble plate assembly over the pistons and into the pump housing. Allow the wobble plate to rest on the pistons.

4. Install the thrust washer over the end of the drive shaft and place the cover over the wobble plate assembly.

Note: The two large inlet openings in the cover go to the bottom of the pump body.

5. Hold the cover, compressed against the wobble plate and pistons springs, in position against the housing and attach with screws.

6. Install new O-rings on the pump body and in the seal groove of the discharge housing. Lubricate only the seal on the pump body.

7. Install the five discharge valves and springs in recesses in the discharge housing.

8. Install the pump body and drive shaft assembly down into the discharge housing. Use a pin or wire to align the valves during the last ¼" of assembly.

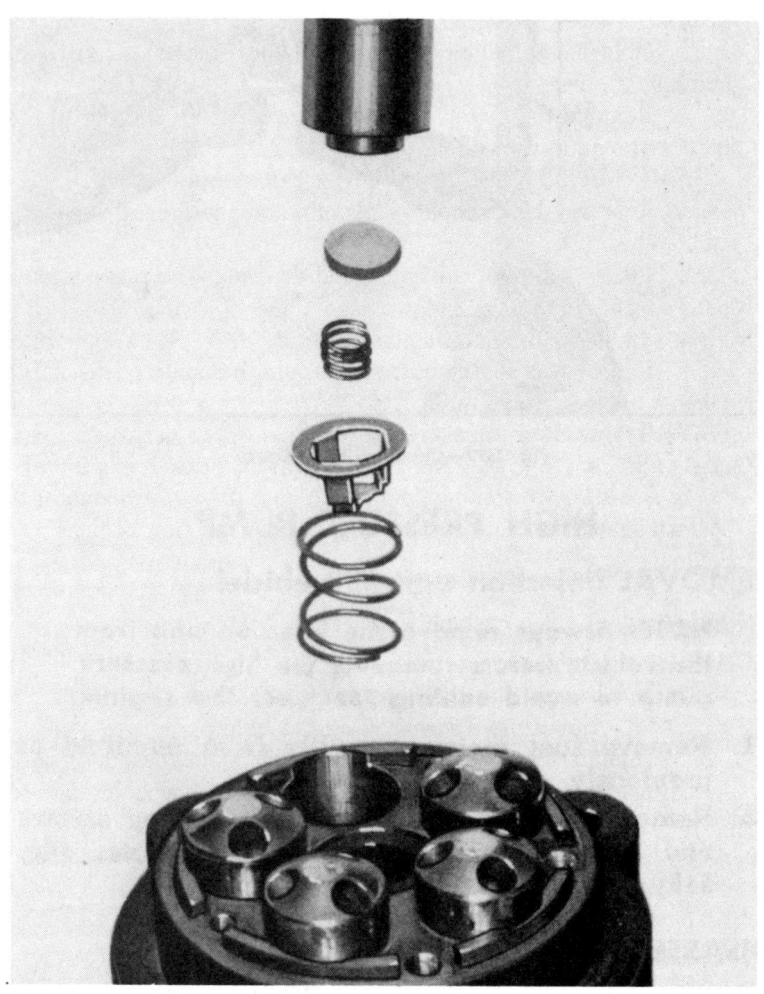

Fig. 3-22. Piston and valve installation.

9. Hold assembly in place and install the two discharge housing-to-pump body screws and lock washer.
10. Install pump and new gasket onto fuel meter.
11. Install fuel meter on manifold.

Intake Manifold

Commonly, the disassembly of the intake manifold and nozzles

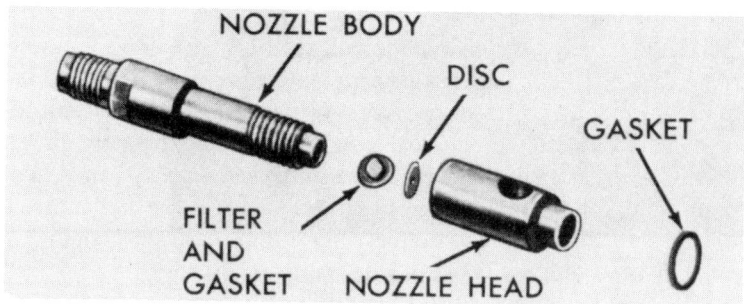

Fig. 3-23. Nozzle assembly exploded view.

is only necessary when a complete overhaul of the injection unit is undertaken.

When cleaning is required, disassemble the manifold down to the bare casting and its ancillary components. Wash in clean solvent and blow dry with compressed air.

Table 3-2. Fuel Injector Nozzles.

Nozzle Code	Part Number
W17 or W18	7017323
W18 or W19	7017324
W19 or W20	7017325

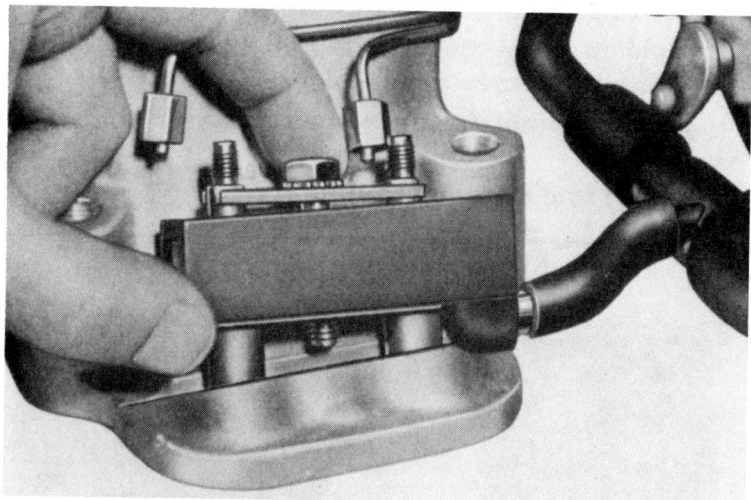

Fig. 3-24. Removing nozzle block assembly.

Nozzle Disassembly & Assembly

Nozzles may be cleaned after disassembly provided that extreme care is used to ensure that reassembly is correct (Fig. 3-23). *Do not* use a wire to clean the nozzle orifice. If necessary, replace the defective nozzle. If one nozzle is found to be extremely dirty, chances are that all of the nozzles are in the same condition. If this condition is found, replace the fuel filter found at the fuel meter. Nozzles are available as complete disassemblies and should be replaced according to Table 3-2.

1. Disconnect and raise the fuel lines out of the way.

Note: Disconnect the throttle bellcrank or fuel pump drive cable and move out of the way while servicing the nozzles.

2. Remove the nozzle block retaining screw and remove nozzle block as an assembly (Fig. 3-24).

3. Remove the nozzles from the nozzle block. Carefully remove the old nozzle gaskets.

4. Hold the nozzle body and insert tool in hand to disassemble the unit.

Note: Use care in disassembly and reassembly. Nozzle orifice discs are assembled with the bright side toward the engine.

5. Clean or replace the nozzle assemblies. Reinstall in the nozzle blocks with new gaskets.

6. To reassemble, reverse steps 1 and 2 (Fig. 3-25).

For additional information and data, see Table 3-3 through 3-6.

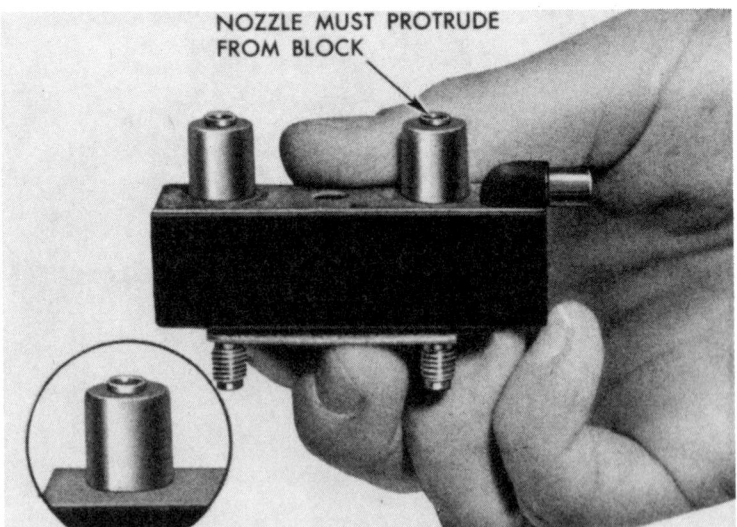

Fig. 3-25. Correct nozzle installation.

Table 3-3. Fuel Injection 1957-1965.

Year	Horsepower	Engine	Fuel Injection Unit
1957	283	Special, mechanical lifters	7014360
1957	283	Special, mechanical lifters	7014520
1957	250	Standard, hydraulic lifters	7014520
1957	250	Standard, hydraulic lifters	7014800
1958	250	Standard, hydraulic lifters	7014800
1957 (late)	250	Standard, hydraulic lifters	7014800R*
1958 (early)	250	Standard, hydraulic lifters	7014800R
1958-59	250	Standard, hydraulic lifters	7014900
1958-59	290	Special, mechanical lifters	7014900R
1957 (late)	283	Special, mechanical lifters	7014960
1958 (early)	290	Special, mechanical lifters	7014960*
1959	250	Standard, hydraulic lifters	7017200
1960-61	275	Standard, hydraulic lifters	7017200
1959	290	Special, mechanical lifters	7017250
1960-61	315	Special, mechanical lifters	7017250
1959	290	Special, mechanical lifters	7017300
1960	315	Special, mechanical lifters	7017300
1960-61	275	Standard, hydraulic lifters	7017310
1960-61	315	Special, mechanical lifters	7017320
1962 (early)	360	Special, mechanical lifters	7017355
1962	360	Special, mechanical lifters	7017360
1963	360	Special, mechanical lifters	7017375
1964 (early)	375	Special, mechanical lifters	7017375R
1964	375	Special, mechanical lifters	7017380
1965	375	Special, mechanical lifters	7017380

* This unit has possible applications for this year

THROTTLE BODY INJECTION FOR 1982

Beginning with the 1982 model year, General Motors resorted to the use of fuel injection once again to solve its performance image in addition to increasing overall fuel economy and lowering exhaust

Table 3-4. Fuel Injection Components.

Injector	Manifold (Plenum)	Adaptor Manifold	Fuel Meter	Air Meter
"Ribbed Top" Small Die Cast Unit				
7014900R	7017033		7017035	7014901
7017200	7017033		7017128	7017201
7017250	7027033		7017129	7017201
"Smooth Top" Small Die Cast Unit				
7017310	7017175	3768233*	7017128	7017201
7017320	7017175	3768233*	7017129	7017201
7017355	7017178	3768233*	7017216	7017356
7017360	7017178	3768233*	7017216	7017356
*Requires distributor spacer lock #3758933				
"Ribbed Top" Large Die Cast Unit				
7017375R	7017309	3826810	7017315	7017376
7017380(1964)	7017391	3826810	7017393	7017381
7017380(1965)	7017391	3826810	7017392	7029539

Table 3-5. Distributor/Fuel Injection Applications.

Distributor	Engine
1110889	1957 (early), 283 hp
1110905	1957, 283 hp
1110906	1957, 1958 (early), 250 hp
1110908	1957 (late), 283 hp
1110914	1958, 1959, 290 hp; 1960, 1961, 315 hp
1110915	1958 (early), 1958, 1959, 250 hp; 1960, 1961, 275 hp
1110916	1958, 250 hp
1110990	1962 (early), 360 hp
1111011	1962, 360 hp
1111022	1963, 360 hp
1111063	1964 (early), 375 hp
1111064	1964, 1965 transistor ignition, option K-66, 375 hp
1111070	1964 (late), 1965, 365 hp

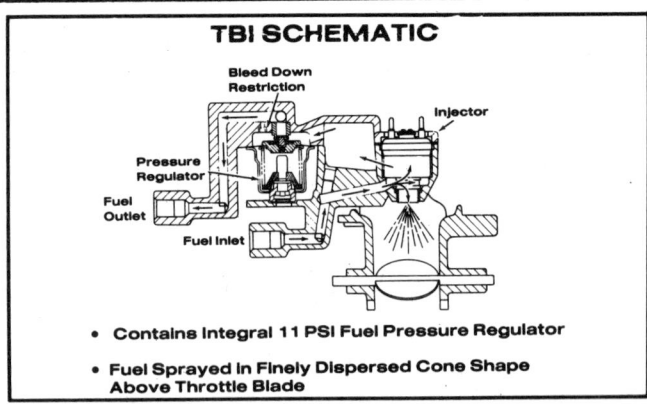

- Contains Integral 11 PSI Fuel Pressure Regulator
- Fuel Sprayed In Finely Dispersed Cone Shape Above Throttle Blade

Fig. 3-26. Fuel injection returned to General Motors and Corvette after an absence of 17 years. Dual exhaust, monolite catalytic converter, and throttle body injection give the 1982 Corvette 200 hp at 4200 rpm.

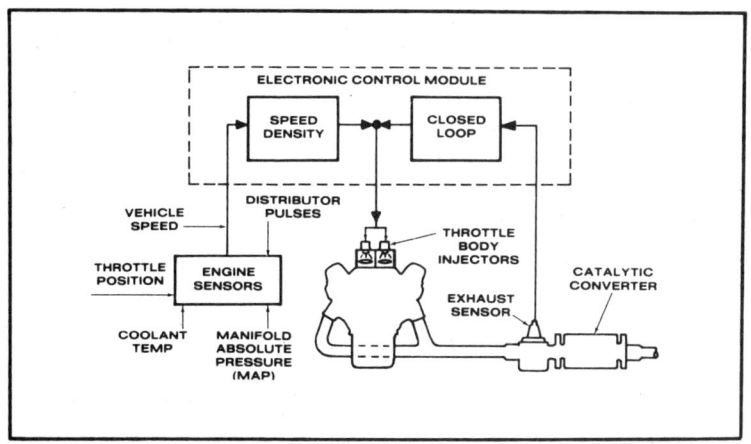

Fig. 3-27. Throttle body injector schematic.

emissions. One of the main reasons for using this type of induction system is that it allows a more precise control of fuel-air ratios over a wider range of operating conditions when compared to a conventional carburetor setup. With this new induction system, horsepower is up to 200@4200 rpm for the 350 c.i. engine; mileage is an estimated 15 mpg for city driving and 26 for highway driving (see Fig. 3-26).

The new fuel injection is a cross-fire injection design—that is, twin throttle body injectors are mounted on tuned crossover man-

Fig. 3-28. The new injection system is a "closed loop" design; that is, the heart of the system is the electronic control module (ECM) which senses and interprets such information as coolant temperature, throttle angle, manifold absolute pressure, engine rpm, and even the completeness of the combustion in the exhaust.

ifold runners, which distribute the fuel/air mixture to opposite sides of the engine. A special "swirl plate" is mounted directly beneath each TBI to insure complete fuel/air mixing (Fig. 3-27). The manifold runner length is 12.5 inches long compared to the old Camaro cross-ram manifold design of 14 inches.

The heart of the new sophisticated system is the on-board computer, the electronic control module (ECM). It is programmed to vary fuel delivery according to the interpretation of a number of factors such as throttle angle, engine rpm, coolant temperature, absolute manifold pressure, and completeness of exhaust combustion (Fig. 3-28). The ECM can adjust the fuel flow 80 times per second compared to 10 times per second with the 1981 carbureted engine.

Chapter 4

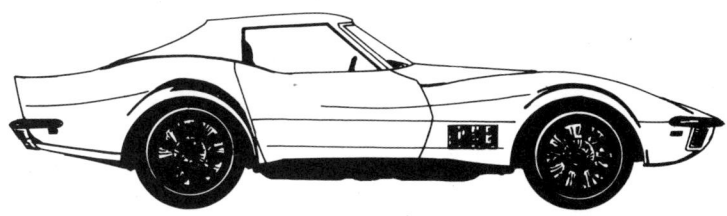

Corvette Disc Brakes

The braking system used on 1953 through 1964 Corvettes features the conventional, industry-wide approach of drum brakes. These operate through internal-expanding, hydraulically operated double piston wheel cylinders. Several options were available throughout their 21-year period: power brakes featuring a Moraine vacuum-assisted master cylinder, metallic brakes with heat-resistant springs, and larger cerametallic linings with finned drums. The latter were principally used on race cars, although they were available as an extra-cost option and therefore could be used on the street if one chose to do so.

In 1965, four-wheel disc brakes were first offered as standard equipment. These consist of a fixed caliper mounted over a rotating disc. The rotors are ventilated, a design feature first used on the GM Firebird II dream car of 1955.

In a paper presented to the Society of Automotive Engineers at the International Automotive Congress in Detroit, Michigan, on January 11-15, 1965, Zora Arkus-Duntov and Arnold R. Brown detailed several guideposts that provided direction for the Corvette disc brake system. The vehicle parameters included a four-wheel disc brake system, minimum change or modification of vehicle design, and true sports car braking performance without power assist. Brake component parameters included fixed and ventilated discs, separate parking brake system, fixed calipers with floating pistons, mandatory splash shields, and heatsink capacity limited only by design.

Although General Motors had been investigating the design of disc brakes for automotive application through its subsidiary, Delco Moraine, since 1937, one major problem was not anticipated—and it has plagued the Corvette disc brake system up through the 1982 model year.

DISC BRAKE PROBLEMS

This inherent design flaw involves the degradation of the braking system through the promotion of rust and corrosion of the cast-iron brake calipers and aluminum brake pistons. Cast iron is a particularly rust-prone metal, especially during periods of inactivity such as dormant winter seasons spent in garage storage. Rusty brake components can result in fluid leaks and possible system failure. What's worse, normal repair methods, such as honing and rebuilding of the cylinders, just are not a permanent cure. In time, the problem can start all over again.

An associated—and perhaps even more severe—problem is that involving the relative movement of the caliper pistons with the disc brake shoes. It appears that this constant-contact design provides for continual friction between these two parts, resulting in the scuffing off of the anodized portion of the piston crown. This, in turn, exposes bare, unprotected aluminum to contact with the steel backing plate of the disc brake shoe. Since the electrical activity of each metal is different, with aluminum being more active, contact between these two metals causes a rapid deterioration of the piston surface. Although only the piston crown will show corrosion, it is possible for the entire piston structure to fail, collapsing inside of the caliper and possibly seizing.

DISC BRAKE SOLUTIONS

Remedies to the braking problems can be through one of three procedures. The first solution comes straight from the General Motors parts department. It seems that during the heyday of the factory racers in the '60s, the road racers demanded greater braking capacity and braking reserve. Thus, one of the brake options made available to them was a high-performance factory option, code number J56. This option consisted of an aluminum brake piston with a special ⅝-inch thick glass-polyester insulator replacing the stock anodized finish found on the standard brake piston crown. Although the original purpose of the modified piston was to dissipate heat under racing conditions, it now serves a double purpose and resists corrosion as well.

The second solution involves the machining and fitting of brass sleeves into the disc brake caliper assembly. This procedure was first developed by White Post Restorations in White Post, Virginia, as an offshoot of its antique auto restoration business. In their business of auto restoration, they had been involved in the process of boring and sleeving antique auto brake cylinders; the Corvette problem seemed to pose little mystery to them. While rusting of the calipers is eliminated through the use of sleeves, the corresponding problem of brake piston corrosion still remains.

The third—and probably the best—solution is available from numerous aftermarket suppliers of Corvette accessories. This cure involves replacing the stock calipers with stainless steel sleeved calipers and matching stainless steel pistons. This idea was originally developed by a professional engineer and long-time sports car enthusiast H. George Jonas. His idea became so successful that he soon started the Stainless Steel Brake Corporation of Clarence, New York, and is today a recognized leader in Corvette rehabilitation.

Stainless steel has numerous advantages over aluminum. It is harder than the anodized aluminum and will therefore not degrade or scuff as can the aluminum. In addition, stainless steel is a poor conductor of heat and will act as an insulator, thereby preventing heat from reaching the rubber seals behind the pistons along with reducing the ambient temperature of the brake fluid. The effect of this thermal insulation is long life for the seals and less chance of brake fluid vapor lock from boiling of the brake fluid.

Caliper replacement is a fairly straightforward and simple procedure. The steps are as follows:

1. Raise and secure the vehicle, preferably through the use of jackstands. With the wheels removed, disconnect the brake hoses running to the front calipers at the support bracket. Disconnect the rear calipers' brake hose from the inboard side of the unit.

2. Tape or plug the end of each brake hose to eliminate the chance of dirt contaminating the system.

3. Remove the cotter pin and the retaining pin and pull out the disc brake shoes. Unbolt the caliper from the mounting bracket.

4. Replace with a reworked caliper using stainless steel sleeves and stainless steel pistons.

5. To assemble, reverse the process.

6. Bleed brake system if necessary.

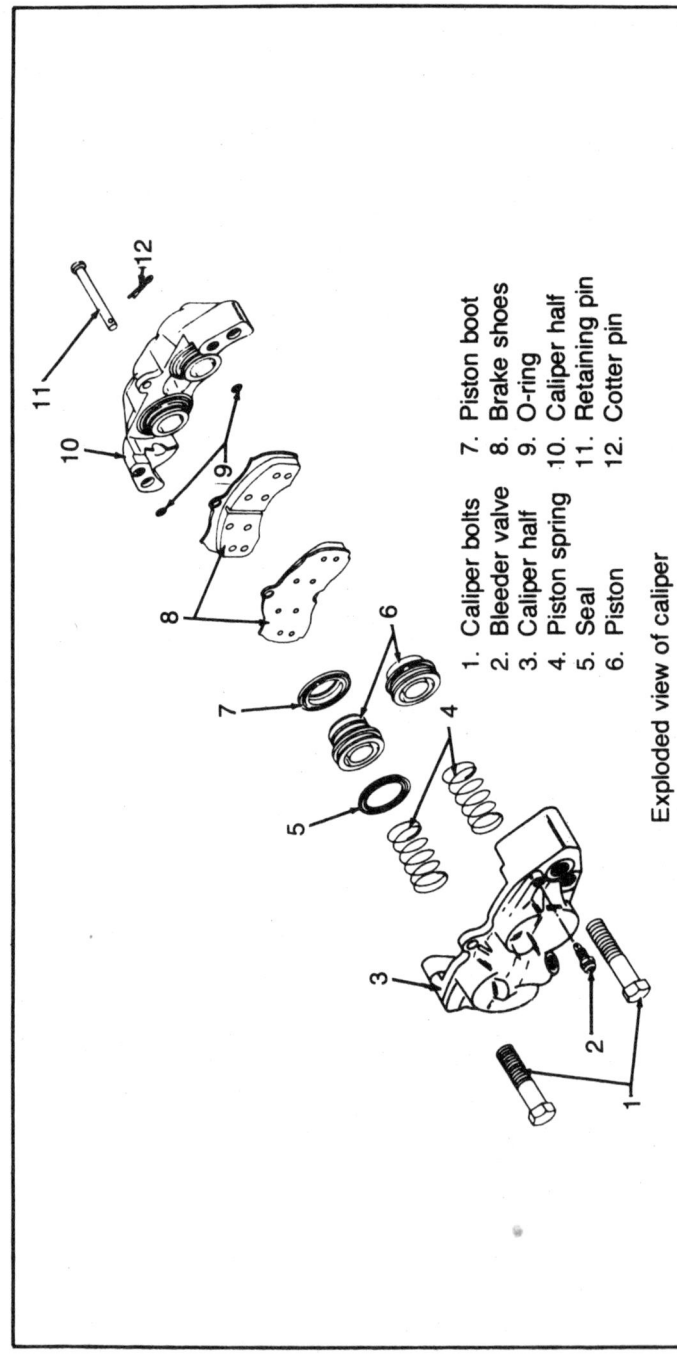

Fig. 4-1. Many aftermarket suppliers of Corvette accessories sell calipers with stainless steel sleeves and matching stainless steel pistons. This setup eliminates the major problem associated with Corvette Delco Moraine disc brakes.

While the braking system is partially disassembled, this is an excellent time to examine the rotors for gouges or severe pitting (Fig. 4-1). Table 4-1 shows the tolerances and torque limits for the Delco Moraine rotors used on Corvettes.

Resurfacing of the rotors may be undertaken if the surface warrants it. However, resurfacing of the rear rotors provides a sizable problem since the critical perpendicular alignment between rotor face and axle centerline may be interrupted. Originally the new rotors and axle shafts were machined at the factory as matched riveted assemblies prior to installation on the chassis. If this alignment is disturbed, air pumping caused by rotor runout can occur.

The problem of rotor runout air pumping is fairly straightforward. Since the caliper pistons are spring-loaded, (i.e., constant contact design), and are always touching the brake shoes, the wobbling rotor causes the pistons to move in and out. In addition, the seals used on the pistons are of a cup-type design; these cause the pistons to become very efficient air pumps, resulting in a loss of pedal on one hand and overflowing the brake fluid in the master cylinder on the other.

Eliminating piston oscillation caused by an out-of-alignment rotor can be accomplished in three ways. First, it may be possible to reposition the rotor in one of the four remaining positions on the axle flange. Moving the rotor to one of these positions, if necessary, requires redrilling of the parking brake adjuster access hole.

Second, if the resurfaced rotor still is not perpendicular to the

Table 4-1. Corvette Disc Brake Specifications, 1965-1980 Delco Moraine.

ROTOR
- Thickness (F & R) .... 1.250 inches
- minimum after re-machining (1971-72) .... 1.230 inches
- minimum allowable .... 1.215 inches
- Parallelism (Total variation in thickness when measured in at least four locations) .... 0.0005 inches
- Lateral runout (1965-70) .... 0.002 inches
- Lateral runout (1971-on) (Maximum rate of change must not exceed 0.001 inch in 30 degrees) .... 0.005 inches
- Surface finish (1965-70) .... 30-50 micro inches
- Surface finish (1971-on) .... 20-60 micro-inches

TORQUE LIMITS
- Caliper mounting bolts (F & R) .... 70 foot-pounds
- Caliper assembly bolts, Front .... 120-140 foot-pounds
- Rear .... 55-65 foot-pounds
- Wheel bearing nut—This procedure can only be done with the friction pads not in contact with the rotor. As wheel rotates, tighten spindle-nut to 12 ft-lbs. Back off the adjusting nut one flat and insert cotter pin. If the slot and pinhole do not align, back off nut ½ turn or less. Rotate wheel to check that it rotates freely, then lock cotter pin in place.

axle after repositioning (as checked by a dial indicator), the rotor and axle shaft can be removed and machined as an assembly, similar to the method used at the initial stage of production.

The third method—and possibly the easiest—is to install Taper Shims, available from Stainless Steel Brakes, mentioned earlier. These patented shims mount over the lug studs and between the axle shaft and rear rotor. They are available in three tapers: .005, .010, and .015 inch.

PARKING BRAKE SOLUTIONS

If corrosion of the primary braking circuit wasn't bad enough, it appears that the parking brake is also prone to corrosion. The parking brake used in conjunction with Corvette disc brakes incorporates a conventional drum braking system within the rotor hub. The actuating mechanism—all mechanically operated parts—are those parts that move and hold fast against the rotor hub. These parts can't be externally lubricated and, consequently, corrode and seize up.

The cure is to replace the frozen parts with either similar parts from GM (which of course can manifest the same problem again at a later date), or to replace the parts with non-corrodible components from aftermarket suppliers. Handbrake kits are readily available and prices for the non-corrodible kits run approximately $35.

Chapter 5

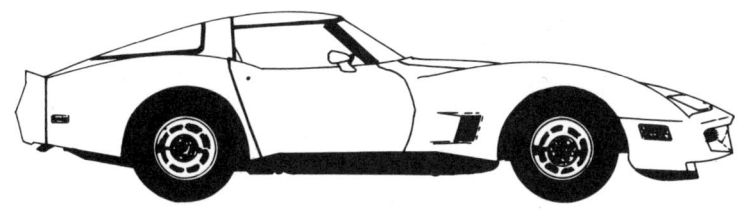

Corvette Restoration Techniques

The complex process of restoring a Corvette is not an undertaking that is contemplated by many people—especially as a ground-up, frame-off project. As the scarcity and value of Corvettes continues to rise, however, the number attempting projects of this nature seems to be increasing yearly.

Prior to undertaking a restoration project of this magnitude, ask yourself these questions—and answer them honestly:

- ☐ Do I really want to take my car off the street for a prolonged period of time?
- ☐ Do I have the financial reserve to complete the project—including any unforeseen costs?
- ☐ Do I have the necessary space and tools?
- ☐ Do I have the knowledge and desire to successfully finish such an undertaking?

You may be surprised at just how many partial restorations have been sold for a fraction of their investment simply because the project was not thought out sufficiently in advance. In fact, this misfortune can often be used to your advantage; parts can usually be picked up at reasonable prices!

If you already have a Corvette in your possession, part of the battle is over. If not, and if restoration and investment are your primary motives, here are a few guidelines and suggestions: make a concerted effort to find your Corvette in as close to original condition as possible. Nothing is more frustrating than trying to determine what came on the car originally. (What is *that* hole for, anyway?) Use restoration manuals such as this one to determine whether or not the equipment on the car actually came with the car from the factory. For example, four-speed transmissions, while listed on the 1957 options list, were actually only available on Corvettes built after May 1, 1957.

RESTORATION METHODOLOGY

Once you have decided to *complete* your restoration (almost everyone wants to *begin* one!), gathering information should be your first priority. Acquire and study restoration guides (again, such as this one), along with highly detailed repair manuals.

One excellent group of manuals is produced by Chevrolet Motor Division. One example is *ST-12, 1953-62 Corvette Servicing Guide.* This three-part guide (body, mechanical, and options) utilizes an I.D. system beginning with general nomenclature, illustrated in Fig. 5-1, and progresses to detailed parts numbers, as shown in Fig. 5-2.

Studying diagrams of parts may not excite you but it is a good way to discover those small problems that suddenly loom up and cause unusual setbacks. Take Fig. 5-3, for example. If you were to glance over the diagram quickly, chances are you would not spend too much time examining the sill plate filler, part number 3726800. With the corresponding parts list and by paying attention to detail, you can discover that this is not a fiberglass part, but one actually constructed of hardwood! Kiln-dried maple, oak, hickory, and ash were used on all 1956-1960 Corvettes. Now imagine finding this part under the sill plate and having to replace it without prior knowledge. It could be quite a time-consuming process finding a duplicate.

In addition to simply identifying parts through the use of exploded diagrams, many pages outline, in quite some detail, instructions for the reassembly of various parts. Figure 5-4, while showing the parts for a driver's door, also indicates how to attach the weather strip and where and what size holes to drill when attaching the door panel. Attention to details such as these are what constitutes exacting, 100-point restorations.

Acquisition of tools is not usually too difficult. Basic hand tools found in the shade-tree mechanic's toolbox do not demand an

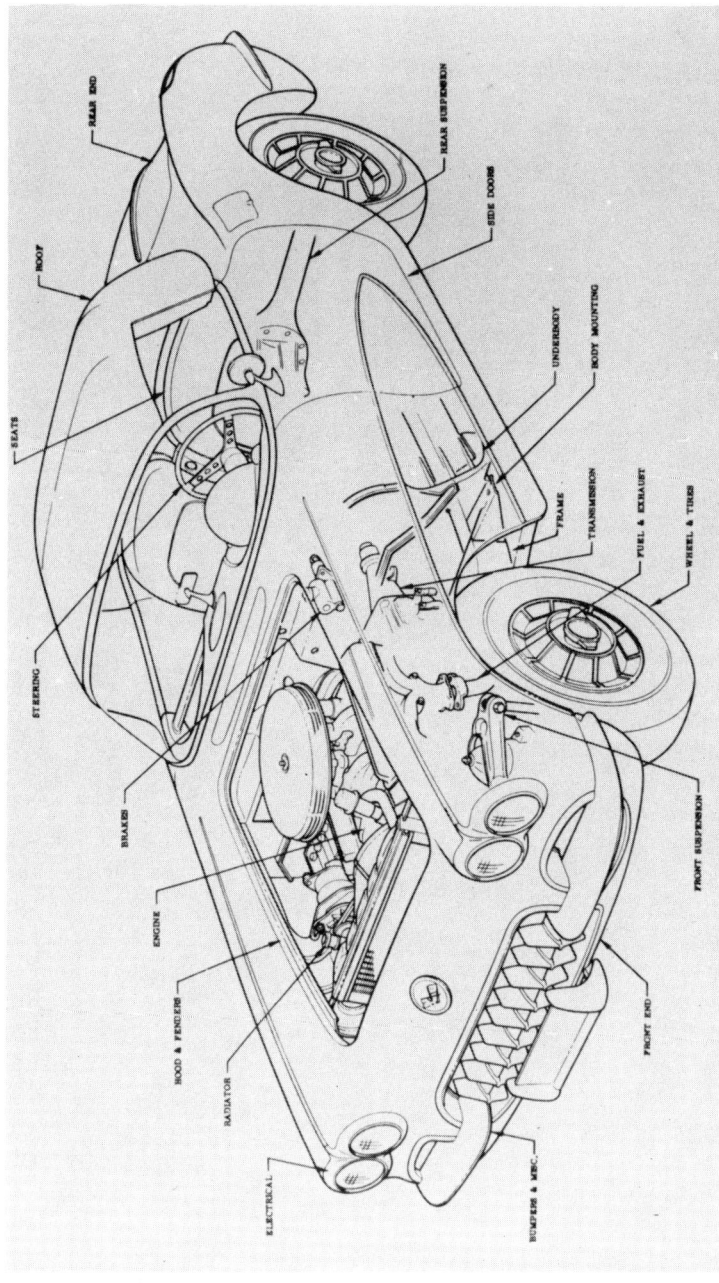

Fig. 5-1. Chevrolet Motor Division offers manuals that can be used by the restorer. These manuals begin with general nomenclature.

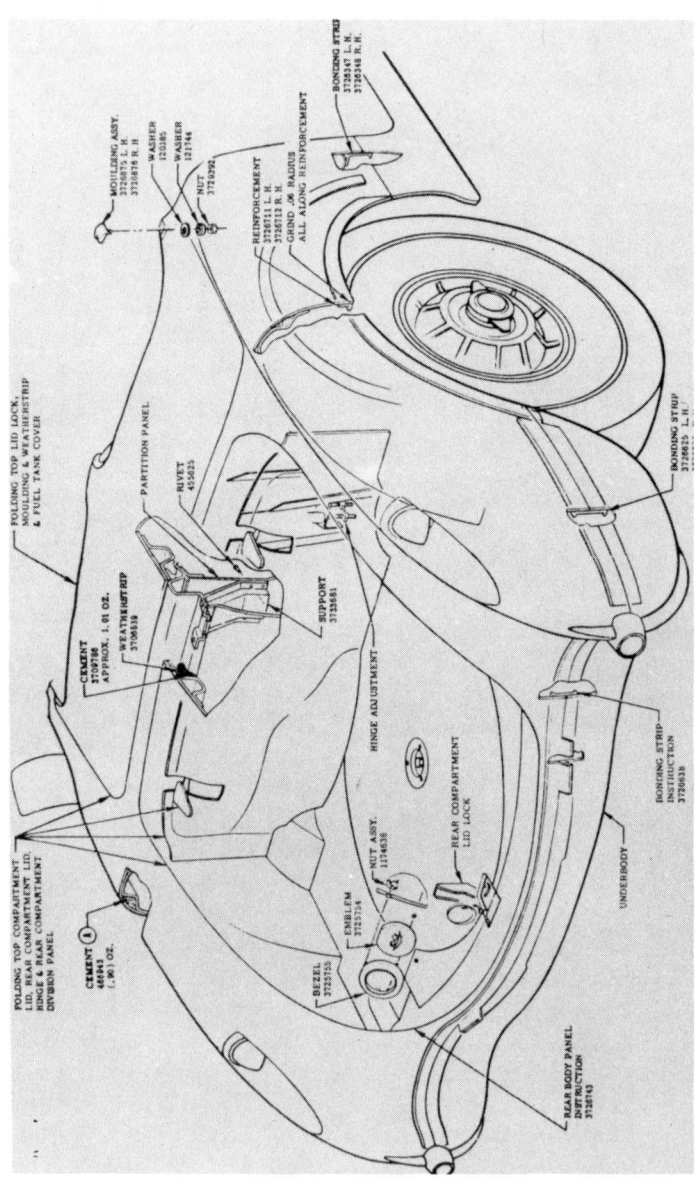

Fig. 5-2. This cutaway drawing illustrates the Uniform Parts Classification ID system. This system details each of these sections and breaks them down into further subdivisions.

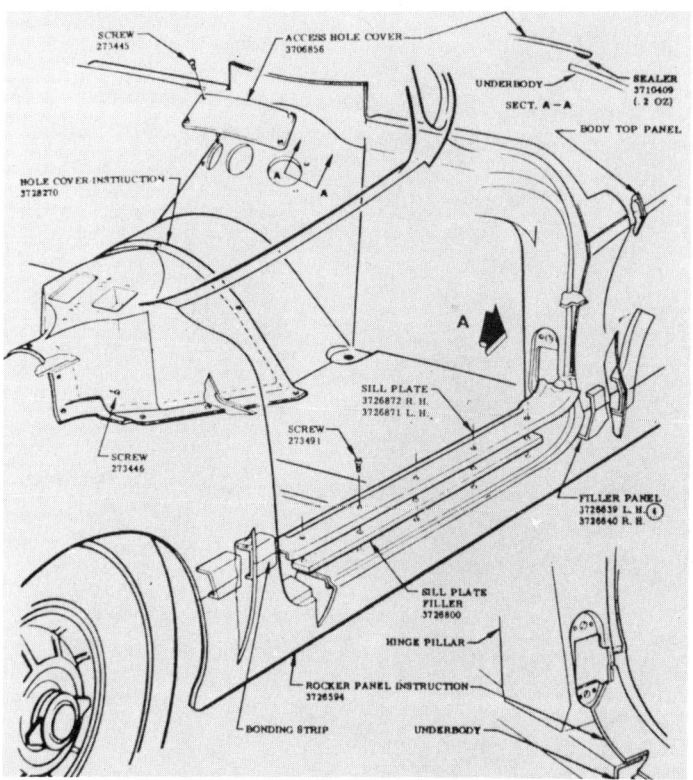

Fig. 5-3. So you thought that all Corvettes were constructed entirely of fiberglass! This illustration shows the sill plate filler, part no. 3726800, which is constructed of kiln-dried hardwood.

exorbitant outlay of cash. Specialty tools (such as ridge reamers, honers, gear pullers, etc.), can be rented in most areas at a fraction of their cost.

After a complete assessment has been made—that is, after the body, engine, and chassis components have been removed and disassembled—conduct an inspection to see which of these parts will require replacement. Don't buy these parts until you are certain you will need them. It shouldn't be too difficult finding most genuine GM replacement parts. The best place for these is still the parts man at your local Chevrolet dealer. Second choice are the numerous swap meets and Corvette club shows throughout the country.

Occasionally some genuine parts are just not available any longer from GM. This is where the repro-parts suppliers enter in. It

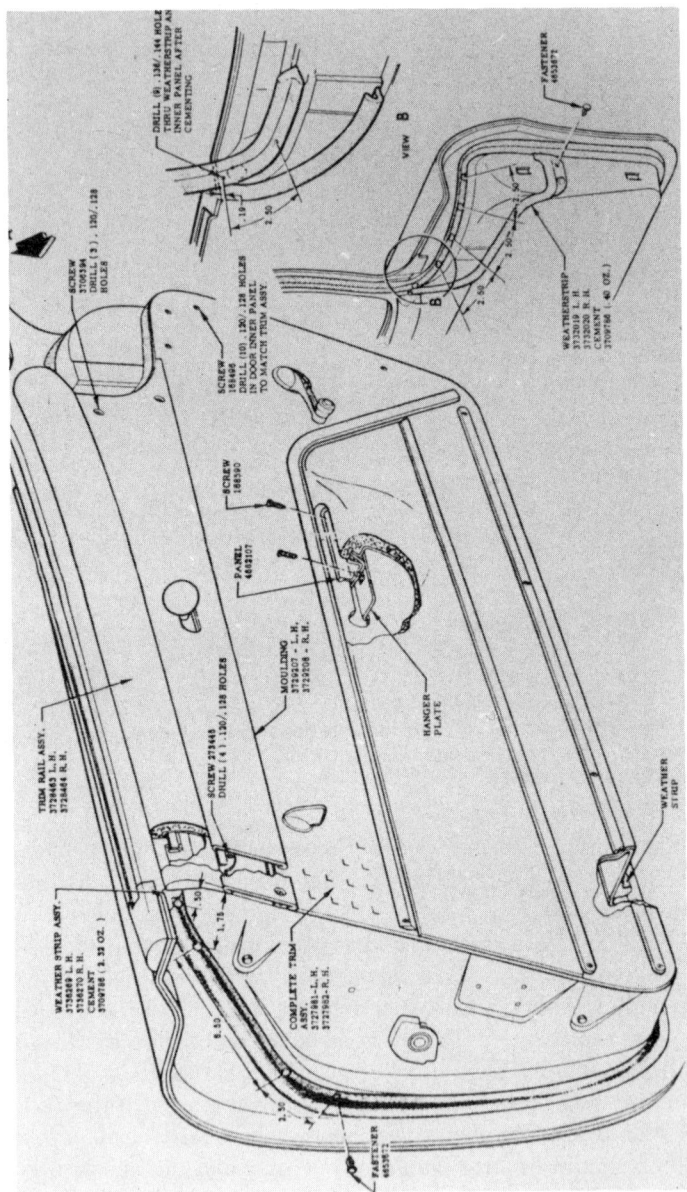

Fig. 5-4. Improved door weatherstrips were introduced on the 1956 models. Instructions for mounting weatherstripping and door panel can be found in this diagram.

is amazing how many seemingly obscure parts are now made by small companies whose sole business is to produce Corvette parts identical to those originally supplied by GM. The list of parts suppliers grows almost monthly.

One of the surest ways to ensuring success on a restoration is to become involved in a car club for that particular marque. Corvette clubs are found throughout the entire U.S. and Canada. At meetings you can learn from other members about how to proceed with a particular step in your restoration, whose parts are best, and perhaps even get a helping hand. In addition, many clubs maintain extensive libraries, so it's not necessary to purchase all of the above-mentioned repair manuals. In short, take advantage of the expertise of others.

One other resource should not go unmentioned. The National Corvette Restorer's Society is an organization dedicated to furthering knowledge about 1953 through 1967 Corvettes. Founded in 1974 by seven men, it has grown into the leading organization disseminating Corvette information. If you own a Corvette from these years or are just simply interested in Corvettes, by all means join the organization. Information can be obtained from NCRS, P.O. Box 81663, Lincoln, NE 68501.

CORVETTE RESTORATION BY GENERAL MOTORS

For many, the ultimate goal of owning a Corvette includes the process of a ground-up restoration. This desire is apparently quite widespread, as evidenced by the large number of repro-parts suppliers, and the fever even crosses corporate boundaries— namely, Chevrolet Motor Division!

The following section details, directly from the project engineer's log, how Chevrolet went about its restoration efforts with their 1953 Corvette. The project began in January 1967 and was completed in April of the same year. A total of 1536 man-hours went into the restoration. The total cost of this restoration is not known since no expense records were kept; at that time no expense was spared and records of this type were not considered necessary— those definitely were the good old days!

The Corvette restoration was initiated in order to put the car on permanent display at GM. This project was necessary because the entire 1953 production run had been completely sold, along with many of the prototypes. Actually, it is believed that the prototypes were destroyed in testing or relegated to obscurity and then destroyed, suffering much the same fate as Corvettes number 001 and 002. (The oldest known Corvette is #3, chassis no. E53F001003.)

In an effort to rectify the situation, Chevrolet decided to locate a 1953 model and restore it to "showroom quality" from the ground up. It was decided to find a car in as near-to-original condition as possible with no modifications. This condition was important because it was felt that there could be problems locating original parts.

Word was sent out to all Chevrolet divisions in late 1966 to be on the lookout for a restorable 1953 Corvette. Within a matter of months several candidates turned up but were eventually rejected because of missing parts or modifications. The project car was finally located on a used car lot in Cincinnati, Ohio. Virtually everything was on the car and intact with the minor exception of an incorrect radio antenna and missing ignition shielding (which surrounds the distributor and spark plugs). The serial number showed the car to be the 225th Corvette built at the Flint, Michigan, plant prior to the move to St. Louis, Missouri.

The car was transported back from Cincinnati to Flint and to the Show and Display Department in Plant 35. Here a tentative schedule, involving 10 steps, was prepared for the project. The steps included:

1. Body removal from the chassis.
2. Engine, chassis, and transmission disassembly.
3. Body component disassembly.
4. Inspection of parts.
5. Procurement of parts.
6. Engine, chassis, and transmission reconstruction.
7. Body and component reconstruction.
8. Reassembly of engine, chassis, and transmission parts as an assembly.
9. Reassembly of body and component parts.
10. Assembly of body and chassis and complete detailing.

The information required for this restoration is supplied in three fundamental publications. Since most of the suspension and brake components are basically the same as the 1953 passenger car, the major reference publication is the *Chevrolet Passenger Car Shop Manual,* 1949-53 (RS-34). The Corvette engine is also basically the same as the standard passenger engine but differs in three areas: the induction system uses three single-barrel carburetors on a special manifold; the exhaust manifold has two outlets for dual exhaust; and the engine utilizes a hotter camshaft. Specific carburetion and ignition data may be found in *Chevrolet Service News,* April and May 1954. Basic body repair procedures are covered in *Corvette Servicing Guide ST-12,* 1962. If this publication is not available, the repair section from the *1963 Corvette Shop Manual* may be used or instructions from various suppliers of fiberglass repair kits should suffice. (Detailed instructions for fiberglass repair also follow in the next chapter.)

The following report is taken from the project engineer's log notebook and follows the steps that Chevrolet used in the restoration of its 1953 Corvette.

Body Removal

- ☐ Six attaching bolts along with the hood hinge stop removed.
- ☐ Carburetor and choke linkage, vacuum and fuel lines removed.
- ☐ Intake manifold taken off (six bolts on the two exhaust pipe flanges and six on the block).
- ☐ Heater and radiator hoses removed and tagged for identification.
- ☐ Car jacked up and placed on wooden supports constructed of 2×4s and plywood, final design 12 inches high.
- ☐ Starter and generator removed and wires tagged.
- ☐ Pitman arm removed from gear shaft along with the three gearbox attaching screws. Most jacket and steering gear remained with the body.
- ☐ Master cylinder drained and brake lines disconnected.
- ☐ Transmission linkage, accelerator linkage, and speedometer cable disconnected.
- ☐ Trunk lid bolts and hinge shims removed and tagged for I.D.
- ☐ Removed engine-to-frame ground wires, license plate light, radio antenna, trunk back panel and parking brake cable at the clevis.
- ☐ Two tail pipe extensions and the battery pan removed. Unbolt the twelve body bolts (two are under the seat cushions).

To this point, after six to eight hours of labor, the body was ready to be lifted from the chassis. The engineering staff decided to attach hooks onto the real bumper brackets inside the trunk. The front lifting points were the hood latch holes. In addition, chainfalls were attached front and rear. The removal was slow in order to feed gas and brake lines, hoses, etc., through the body openings as the body was being raised. After the body was removed from the chassis, it was situated on a four-wheel buggy with braces underneath at the approximate center of the front and rear wheel wells and a support in the center of the body. These, it was felt, would keep the body from sagging.

Frame-to-body mount rubber pads were removed and tagged to use for future assembly (Fig. 5-5). The original order is important so that the body panels along with the doors, hood, and trunk will fit properly.

At this pint the chassis was moved to the steam-cleaning booth to remove the years of accumulated dirt and grime. The hot steam also removed a lot of paint, making futher disassembly easier.

The removal of the body now made the disassembly and removal of the engine and transmission much easier. These were taken out as a unit by first removing miscellaneous parts such as the fuel pump, distributor, fuel line, rocker cover, radiator overflow tank, transmission dipstick and tube, tappet side cover, breather pipe assembly, cylinder head, pushrods, front propeller shaft and U-joint, engine and transmission mount bolts.

Engine and Transmission Removal and Inspection

- ☐ Two lifting eyebolts were attached to the front and rear head bolts with the chainfall attached to a chain between the eyebolts.
- ☐ Transmission removed from engine.
- ☐ Engine dismantled in following order: oil pan, pistons and rods, tappets, oil pump, fan, water pump, fan and crankshaft pulleys, timing gear cover, camshaft and timing gear assembly, engine front mounting plate, flywheel, water outlet and thermostat. The main bearing caps and crankshaft were also removed.

At this point detailed checks and inspection of parts could begin. Cylinder bores were found to be within acceptable wear limits.

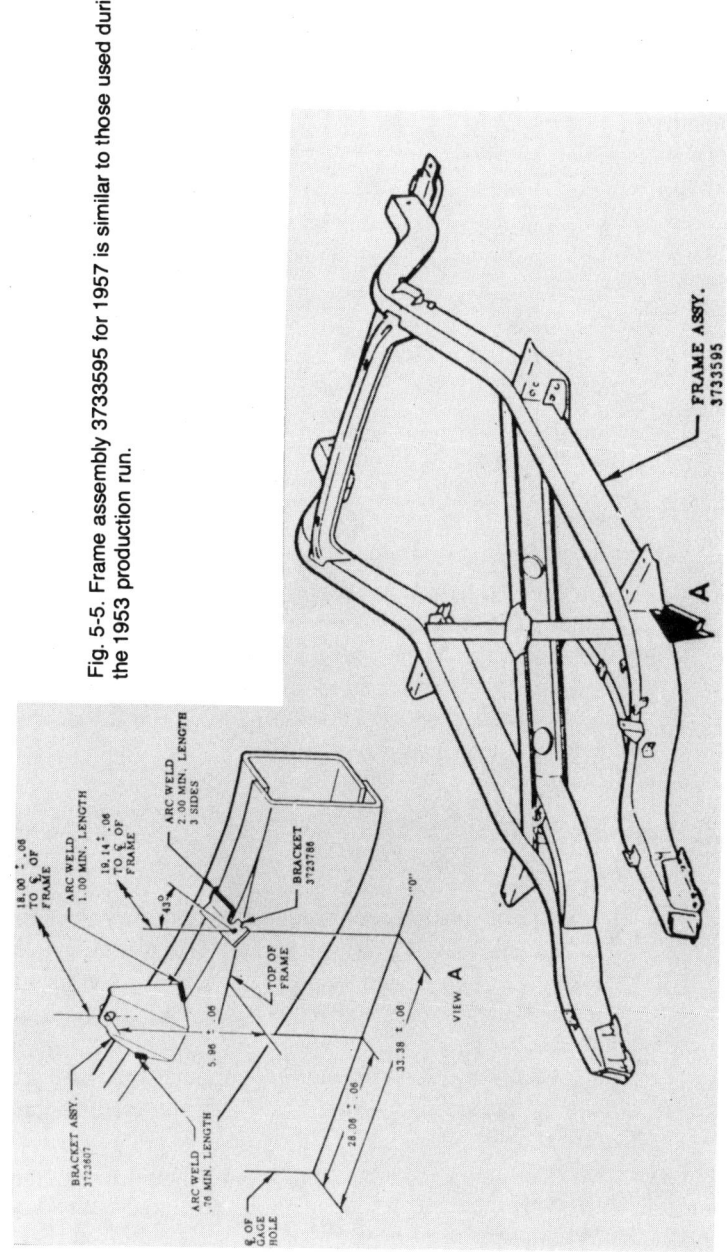

Fig. 5-5. Frame assembly 3733595 for 1957 is similar to those used during the 1953 production run.

- ☐ Block checked and found to be satisfactory.
- ☐ Camshaft and crankshaft checked and found within wear limits.
- ☐ Pistons found to have slight evidence of scuffing so all six were replaced along with piston rings.
- ☐ Connecting rods checked for alignment and found satisfactory.
- ☐ Timing gear found to be worn and replaced.
- ☐ Cylinder head dismantled by removing valve keepers, spring caps, springs, and valves.
- ☐ Cylinder head components checked, valve springs replaced, six were found weak. Valves themselves appeared good and required only grinding along with the seats. Valve guides scheduled for replacement.
- ☐ Cleaned and checked Carter carburetors (YH 2066-SA). Cleaned all parts and decided to try and find repair kit to rebuild.
- ☐ Exhaust and intake manifolds checked; one broken stud required drilling and tapping.
- ☐ Powerglide transmission examined for wear by visual inspection. The unit had been operating normally prior to restoration; no "burnt cork" smell or obvious wear. Replaced pan gasket and painted with Dulex semigloss black.
- ☐ Generator and starter disassembled and rebuilt with new brushes and bearings.

Disassembly of Chassis

- ☐ The front suspension was removed as an entire assembly with the removal of 16 nuts and bolts. Also had to undo the brake lines, hoses and clips, two stabilizer brackets, steering linkage, tire and wheel assemblies, and brake components (Fig. 5-6).
- ☐ Control arms and steering knuckle supports removed after collapsing the springs. Shock absorbers and backing plates also removed.
- ☐ Brake cylinders, lines, and hoses checked for wear. Kingpins and bushings looked good and reused. Shock absorbers appeared to be original and were replaced. Brake

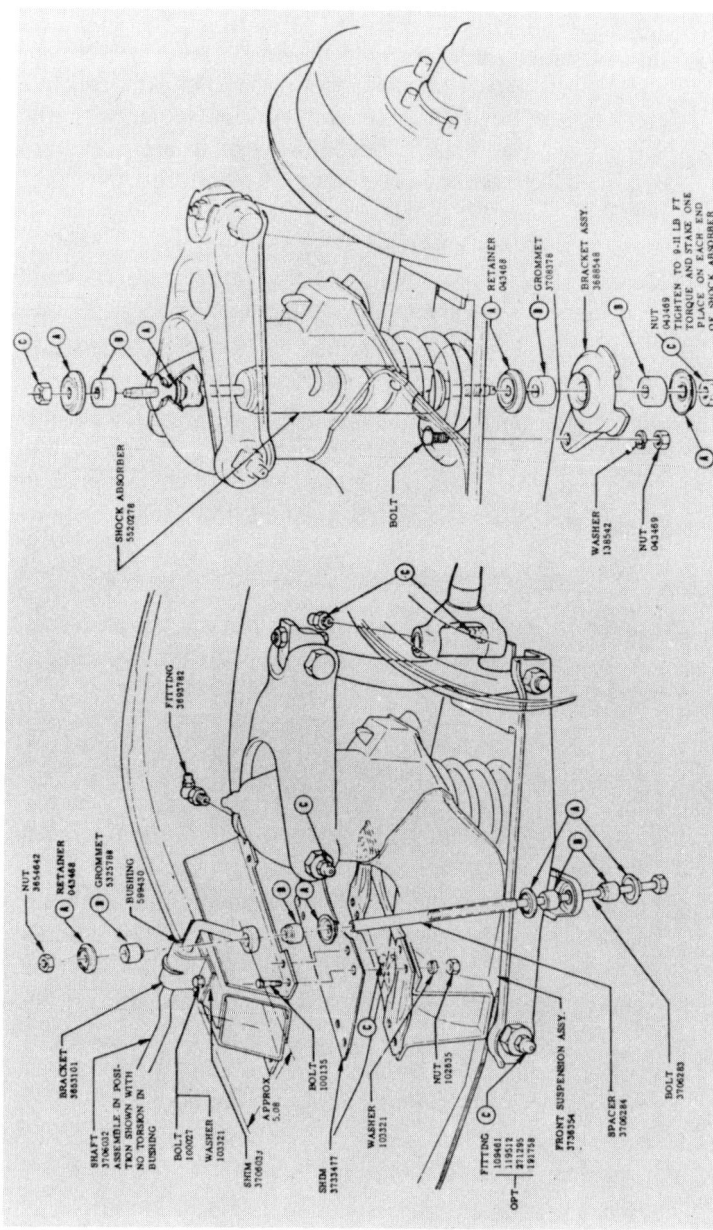

Fig. 5-6. Early Corvette front suspension assembly.

- ☐ drums checked for scoring; they appeared to have been turned once, although they are fine for reuse.
- ☐ Rear suspension also removed as an assembly. Items removed: brake cable brackets, hydraulic lines at T fitting, shock absorbers, front and rear spring hangers, rebound straps, U-bolts, rear axle and springs along with the driveshaft. Many nuts and bolts were frozen and were heated to facilitate removal; however, some still broke (Fig. 5-7).
- ☐ Rear axle cover removed for inspection of differential. Excessive play was found and the gears were replaced according to standard workshop procedures.
- ☐ Some spring leaves were found to be broken and the entire spring assembly was replaced.
- ☐ Bare frame taken for sandblasting. Afterwards, all welds were checked and rewelded if necessary. The frame was repainted with Dulex semigloss black. All chassis components were repainted with the same paint before reassembly.

Concurrent with the mechanical restoration was the disassembly of the body and interior. No particular set pattern was used, just what seemed logical.

- ☐ Taillight assemblies removed along with the trunk floor panel. This gave access to the rear bumpers and guards. Some of the nuts had become embedded in the fiberglass over the years.
- ☐ Light screens from the headlights removed, then the headlight units and housings. (Decided to use plated machine screws when reassembling.)
- ☐ Removed front bumper and guard attachments. Rusted nuts cut with torch.
- ☐ Very carefully pried the bezels from around the exhaust pipes in order to prevent damage to the body.
- ☐ Removed inner door moldings (trim panels) to get at the upper door outer moldings.
- ☐ Window moldings, upper door moldings, convertible top cover trim moldings cover, top, window moldings, top

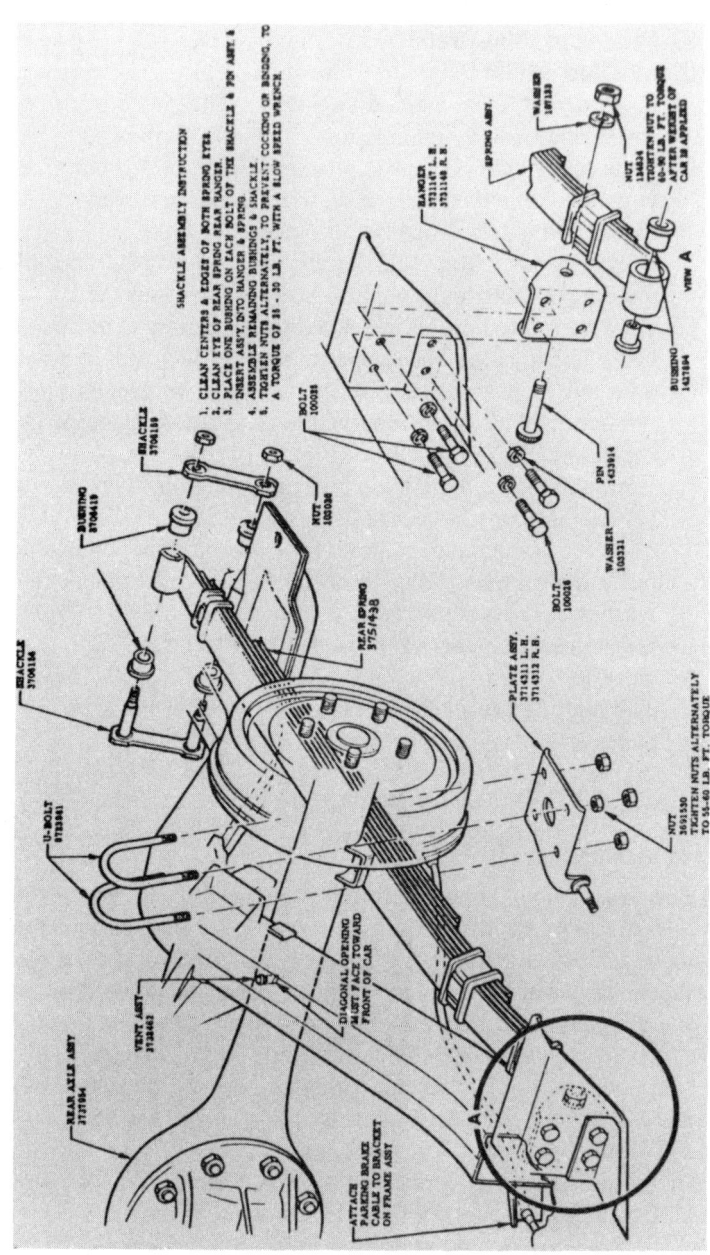

Fig. 5-7. Early Corvette rear suspension assembly.

cover catch, trim around seat edge, and seat divider trim removed.
- ☐ Fender moldings removed.
- ☐ Molding behind the doors removed and at this time it was noticed that they needed replacing. The old ones were saved and used as models for handmade duplicates.
- ☐ Radiator rubber splash guard and 16 retaining bolts removed holding the radiator support. Grille removed; noted that it had cracked in several places.
- ☐ Horns, front "Corvette" emblem, seat backs, doorsill moldings, windshield wipers, and carpet taken out.
- ☐ Prior to removing the windshield, the radio and defroster bezel had to come out. Upper and lower windshield moldings and upper and lower windshield trim pieces were removed. Windshield removed next and it was decided to replace it upon installation (Fig. 5-8).
- ☐ Horn hub insert, horn ring, steering wheel hub and assembly along with the bearings removed. Inside rear view mirror, instrument panel front rail, left and right windshield posts and moldings, left and right doors, and windshield washer nozzles removed.
- ☐ Since the instruments appeared good and worked well, they were left intact.
- ☐ The body is now completely stripped of interfacing components and ready for restoration.

Body Rehabilitation

The first step in the restoration was the preparation of the body. All of the wax and grease accumulated over the years had to be removed; this was done by wiping the body with Prep-Sol, a wax and silicone remover. This must be done prior to sanding since the wax and silicone could become embedded in the finish and would cause further problems such as paint lifting, etc., later on.

Open-coat #240-grit silicone-carbide sandpaper was used over the entire body with a hand vibrator. Cracked and crazed paint was sanded to bare fiberglass. The body was dusted and sprayed with lacquer thinner in order to make scratches and fine cracks more visible. Cracks were enlarged with a rotary file to make them easier for repair. The cracks smoothed with #240-grit paper.

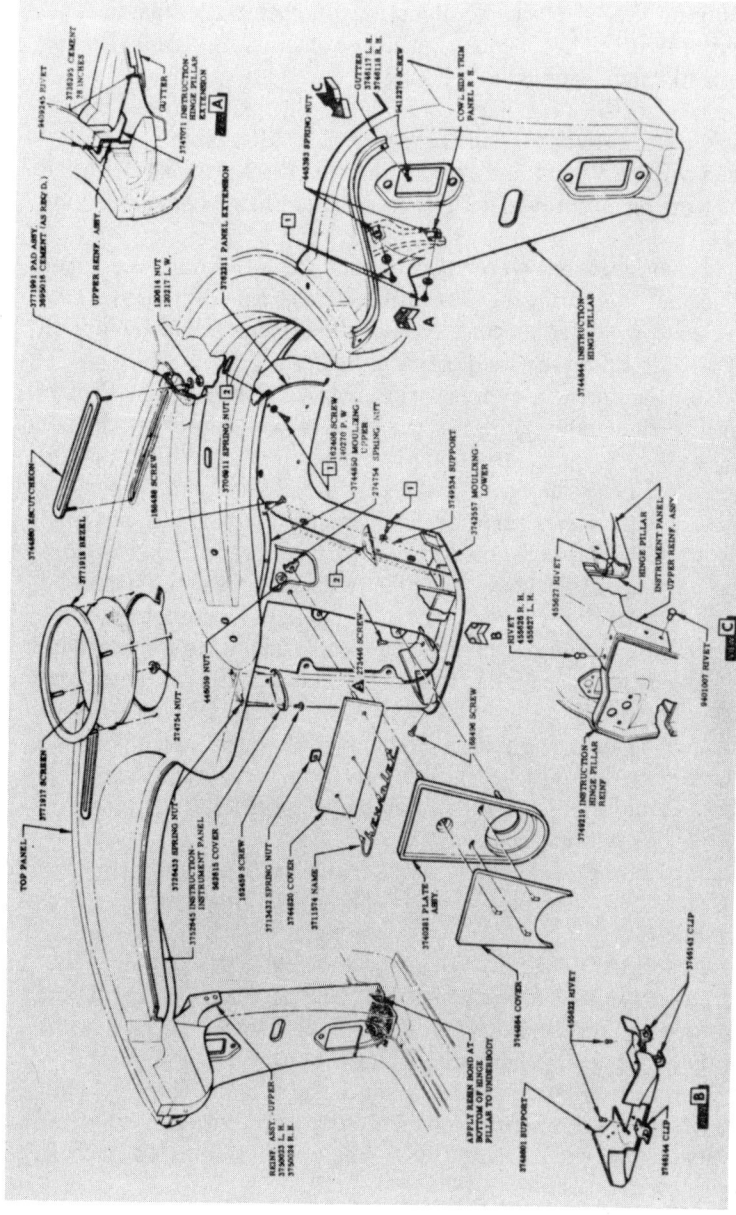

Fig. 5-8. Items such as the top panel and escutcheons are easier to replace when the windshield is removed.

All cracks and damaged areas were filled with Ren Epoxy, from Ren Plastics, Lansing, MI. The material comes in two containers; the mixture is a 50-50 combination of each. The plastic was smoothed with cloth soaked in denatured alcohol. The alcohol keeps the plastic substance from sticking to the cloth.

Prior to the final hardening stage, the plastic filler can be shaved to form to reduce final sanding. The filled area was rough-sanded with #80-grit and resanded with #240-grit. The worked areas were again sprayed with lacquer thinner to spot any remaining cracks.

All worked areas were checked to make certain that the edges had perfect feathering between filled areas and the surrounding fiberglass/primer/color coat. All worked areas were sprayed with Co-Polymer Epoxy Enamel Sanding Sealer.

Now the entire body was sprayed with Rinshed-Mason Primer Surfacer, then wet-sanded with #320-A waterproof sandpaper using plenty of water. Any body imperfections were filled in with Green Stuff body filler and resanded with #320-A wet paper and respotted with primer surfacer. This process of final filler, sanding, and repriming was continued until a surface free of imperfections was obtained. A final coat of primer and sealer was then applied.

At this stage the color coats were applied. Duco Polo white, a nitrocellulose lacquer, was used to closely duplicate the original. The fresh paint was baked in a drying chamber at 200° for about four hours. The final color coat was color sanded with #600-A sandpaper, again using plenty of water. The water was squeegeed off during final sanding to check for any minor imperfections. (The surface should look dull with small shiny specks left for final buffing.) During the final inspection, many cracks would reappear and the task of filling, sanding, sealing, priming and painting would be necessary. It was decided to leave the final buffing until after final assembly:

All soft trim was removed from the seats, door panels, etc., and used as patterns for new material. The wire stays were marked for re-use and the seat cushion underpinnings were redone, some with new coil springs and all with new burlap.

The same treatment was given to the top and carpets. They were cut apart at the seams and used as patterns with new material. The seats received new red vinyl which was assembled in these stages:

☐ New padding placed over cushion spring frame, attached

with hog rings and wire stays.
- [ ] Foam rubber attached over padding; reshaped seat with additional padding.
- [ ] Attached new vinyl with hog rings.
- [ ] Removed wrinkles with a hair dryer; kneaded looseness out.

The carpeting was loosely fitted into the vehicle before final sewing and binding. All chrome trim, including many new pieces, were sent to Davison Plating Company and the Saginaw Plating Company to be "show quality" chromed. The original pieces were sent to the shop when new ones were not available.

The ignition shielding originally installed on the car was not deemed acceptable for re-use so it was decided to obtain original diagrams of the shielding and have it reproduced by outside sources. The estimates received were extremely high, so the shielding was formed out of thin plastic since this was to be a "show car;" the real item would not be necessary because the car would not be driven on the street.

Reassembly

In general, reassembly is the reverse of disassembly. As the old components were renewed, they were installed when possible. By the time the body work was well along, most of the chassis work had been completed and the running gear installed.

- [ ] Engine: Received new pistons, rods and bearings. The valves were ground and new valve springs installed. Carburetors were rebuilt. New hoses, thermostat, fuel pump, wiring, and distributor were installed. All parts to be painted were redone with the correct blue enamel.
- [ ] Transmission: All parts of the Powerglide appeared to be in perfect order. Front and rear seals were installed and it was painted with Dulex semigloss enamel.
- [ ] Rear axle and suspension: The gears in the differential carrier were replaced along with new shocks and springs. The entire assembly was painted with semigloss enamel.
- [ ] Frame, steering, and front suspension: Despite the age of the suspension components, most parts appeared to be in good shape and were re-used; only the steering gears were replaced along with the shocks. Repainted with semigloss enamel.

- ☐ Body and components: Every item removed from the car was either replaced or renewed to bring it up to new-car status. The steering wheel was repainted but the horn ring, emblem, etc., were replaced with new stock as were the windshield and interior parts. The chrome pieces were all mostly new and were replated to "show quality."
- ☐ Before the body was installed on the rolling chassis, all of the refurbished components were returned to their original locations. By now the body could be mated to the chassis with care taken to ensure that the shims that were removed were returned to their original locations.
- ☐ All hoses, brake lines and cables, shift linkage, throttle linkage, wire connectors, and other miscellaneous parts were installed.
- ☐ Added oil, water, and fuel.
- ☐ Resanded, filled, sealed, primed, and painted all nicked and damaged areas encountered during the final body fitting.

The final operation was to drive the finished Corvette restoration to a waiting van to take it to Detroit.

Chapter 6

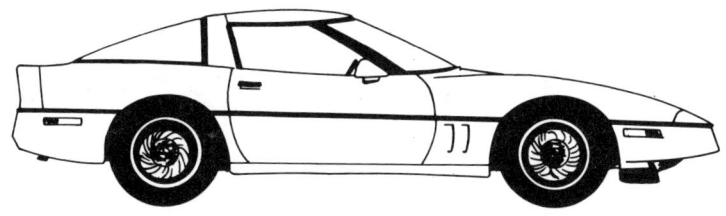

Corvette Fiberglass Repair and Repainting

With the movement afoot for do-it-yourself projects, more and more people are taking on the task of doing their own body repair, even with fiberglass cars. Fiberglass is actually quicker and easier to repair at home than similarly damaged steel. By adhering to the manufacturers' directions supplied with the various products, and by following the information below, excellent results can be obtained that can rival almost any body shop.

Prior to any actual fiberglass repair, it may become necessary to repair structural damage done to the steel parts that underlie certain fiberglass panels. When welding these parts, care must be taken to keep the flame or heat from the welder from coming in direct contact with the surrounding fiberglass. An excellent way to avoid this is to use an application of wet asbestos sheets or several layers of aluminum foil as a heat shield.

Another caution—which many seem to overlook—is checking behind the area being worked on for damage to electrical wires, motors, cables, and similar items. Once repair work is completed, it is often difficult or actually impossible to gain access to that same area. If there is a problem, get it while it's handy.

With the steel structural cages used for passenger protection in the 1963 and newer bodies (Fig. 6-1), damage is usually such that the framework must be straightened. This must be done with care if the steel members are still in the body. When using hydraulic jacks it must be kept in mind that the jack is exerting force opposite the

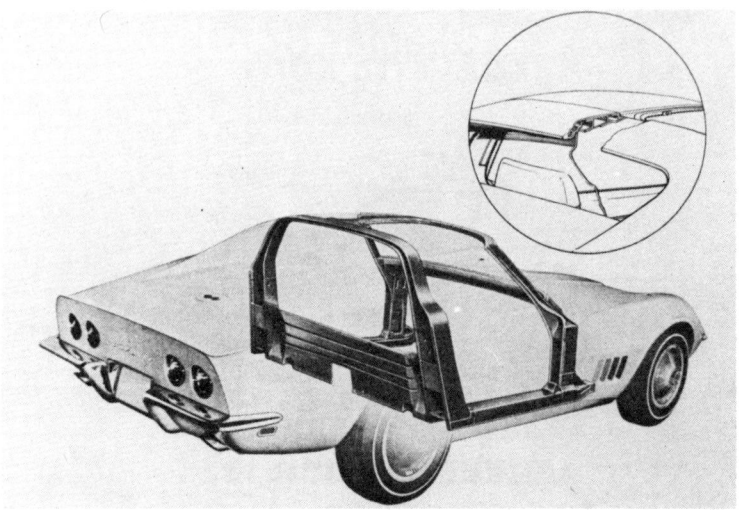

Fig. 6-1. Steel reinforcement beams in the second and third generation Corvettes make it mandatory that care and precision are used when making repairs to them. Welding and straightening must be done carefully.

intended area and that area must be able to take that stress. Fiberglass parts cannot be straightened, so if poor body alignment exists or persists, check the steel reinforcements in the sub-panel areas.

Before using any fiberglass repair products, take care that the chances of skin irritation are kept at a minimum. Occupational or contact dermatitis is an irritation that results in people who have a tendency towards irritation from the resins or dust. In many kits, creams are supplied to counteract these skin problems. Most people will not need to use the creams except when working with fiberglass cloth or mat, as the fibers from these materials actually embed themselves in the skin.

In addition to the fiberglass precautions, care should be taken when working with sanders and grinders.

Here is a list of precautions suggested by Chevrolet when working with fiberglass repair kits:

- ☐ Use protective creams when working with fiberglass repair kits.
- ☐ Remove the resin mixture as soon as possible and definitely before it begins to harden. Resin may be removed with lacquer thinner, followed by thoroughly washing the hands.

- ☐ Some type of facial respirator designed to restrict toxic vapors should be worn. Remember, resin vapors may be toxic, so they should be used in a well-ventilated area.
- ☐ Use a sander with some sort of vacuum attachment to control dust.
- ☐ Keep your work area, materials, and utensils clean and dry. The bonding process involved with many of the repair kits relies on chemical reactions, and dirt or moisture may adversely affect these chemical balances.
- ☐ Before beginning any repair work, check for hidden damage to other areas by looking for hairline cracks, applying pressure to surrounding panels, etc. This can possibly prevent extensive repair work in the future.

When planning any repair procedure involving the fiberglass Corvette body, you should know that Chevrolet made a change in body materials beginning in 1971. These changes determine which type of body repair kit is required. We'll cover these in a minute, but first, a short history of Corvette body materials.

As mentioned earlier, most early Corvette body parts were contracted out by Chevrolet to various fiberglass parts companies. Chief among these was one of the original vendors, Robert S. Morrison, founder of Molded Fiber Glass Body Company. He set the specifications of the fiberglass for strength, fiberglass content, surface characteristics, and thickness (.100″).

As Corvette sales and production rose, Chevrolet began to look for new ways to produce smoother finishes while at the same time lowering the cost of manufacturing the car. At this time several other companies became involved in the body parts supply business and the introduction of cheap fillers—clay and limestone—soon appeared. These low-profile resin additives reduced the cost while providing a smoother finish, although this was ultimately achieved at the expense of reducing the amount of glass fiber.

The reason inert fillers produce a smoother finish and are used is fairly complicated, but the fundamental action is as follows: Normal polyester resins shrink during the curing and drying process. Unsaturated molecules of maleic anbydride cross-link with styrene monomer; this results in a cured resin taking up six to eight percent less space than uncured liquid resin. The addition of inert fillers reduces the shrinkage rate, although too much filler reduces strength as well.

At some point during the '60s it was discovered that by adding a thermoplastic polymer (such as methyl methacrylate) to a polyester resin, shrinkage was reduced greatly. It acts similarly to other inert fillers but does not cross-link with the resin; it merely swells up.

According to Robert S. Morrison, parts made with these low-shrink resins are weaker, especially in the areas of painting quality, adhesion of bonding materials, and reverse impact. He feels that Chevrolet moved to these manufacturing techniques because of cost-saving benefits.

The change to inert resin fillers was only the first step in the evolution of plastic body parts for the Corvette. The next (and current) process of producing Corvette bodies is called SMC—fiberglass reinforced sheet molding compound. SMC was developed in the late '60s along with the low-shrink resins; the result is low-profile SMC.

SMC was first used in the Corvette in 1970 with selected panels. However, more and more parts were produced by this method in 1971 and 1972; by 1973, over 90 percent of the fiberglass parts used on the Corvette were made from SMC.

Sheet molding compound is produced by coating a lower and upper layer of polyethylene film with a highly filled polyester resin to which a thickening agent has been added. One-inch fiberglass strands are then dropped on the resin on the lower film and the two films are sandwiched together through a series of rollers that squeeze out all of the trapped air. These layers are then rolled up into bundles and put in an 85° F maturing room for about 96 hours. The resin thickens up to the point that when it is placed in a set of dies in a high-pressure press, the glass fibers and resin are pushed into every space in the cavity.

The primary advantage of SMC over perform or mat molding is that it requires a less skilled operator to produce a good-looking part. In addition, changes in bosses and section thickness can be accomplished where they cannot with mat or preform.

Now where does this leave us relative to fiberglass repair? Chevrolet offers four types of repair kits for Corvette repair. They are the Resin Repair Kit, Plastic Solder Repair Kit, Liquid Epoxy Repair Kit, and Epoxy Solder-Adhesive Kit. The first two are for use with Corvette bodies prior to 1971; the last two are specifically designed for use with SMC body parts.

While it is possible for the epoxy-based kit to be used successfully on pre-1971 Corvettes, the two polyester-based kits cannot be used on post-1971 Corvettes. In fact, the conception of the epoxy kit originated when Chevrolet began to receive complaints that the polyester-based kits, which had been used for all repairs in the past, were not providing long-lasting repairs.

REPAIR PROCEDURES

Fiberglass repair procedures for all Corvettes can be divided into two general categories: cosmetic repairs (i.e., scratched panels, dents or pits, cracks in the glaze coat, small holes in the panels) and structural repairs (i.e., large holes, fractured panels, cracks at panel junctions). These two general categories use different repair kits and each type of fiberglass—polyester-based resin and SMC—has its own type of fiberglass repair kit. Consequently, we will be discussing in this section four types of repair kits for Corvette fiberglass repair.

Cosmetic repairs can be made fairly easily with the following two kits. For pre-1971 Corvettes—those with polyester-based resin fiberglass—The Plastic Solder Repair Kit, part no. 1051383, is the one to use. Post-1971 SMC-paneled Corvettes require the Epoxy Solder-Adhesive Repair Kit, part no. 1051885.

Structural repairs, which may require replacement panels in addition to the kits, are made by using the Resin Repair Kit for earlier, polyester based resin Corvettes, and the Liquid Epoxy Resin Repair Kit, part no. 1051906, for newer SMC-bodied Corvettes. Again, these are separate applications, but the Liquid Epoxy Resin Repair Kit can be applied to *all* Corvettes, old and new, while the Resin Repair Kit can only be used on pre-1971 models.

Although the kits are designed for application on different types of fiberglass, they do have similar mixing instructions and the directions for use are identical.

Cosmetic Repair

Use Plastic Solder Repair Kit, PN 1051383, or Epoxy Solder-Adhesive Repair Kit, PN 1051885.

1. Remove all paint surrounding the area down to the laminate. Carefully inspect the area for any hidden damage, such as cracks, holes, etc.

2. Using 220-grit wet-or-dry sandpaper, feather-edge the repair area in the surrounding paint.

3. If the damaged area extends into the laminate, grind or file depression into a V shape. Scuff-sand this section of the repair area so the plastic solder will be able to adhere well.

4. Mix the Plastic Solder or Epoxy Solder-Adhesive using one part solder to one part hardener. Be certain to mix the two substances well.

5. Apply the material with a large putty knife or a rubber squeegee, laying a liberal amount on the damaged area. Build up to the desired thickness making certain that a slight amount more than necessary is used to create a slight dome. Remember, the excess filler can always be removed once it has begun to set up.

6. Deep filling and vertical surfaces may require several layers. Each of the layers should not exceed ½ inch thick.

7. Curing is recommended by using a heat lamp placed at least 12 inches away from the repaired spot for approximately 15 to 20 minutes; the repair will cure faster and will result in a stronger bond. Room temperature curing can also be employed and should occur for at least eight to ten hours or according to directions with the kit.

8. Once the repaired area has cured, grind, sand, and block-sand before priming and applying the final color coat.

Structural Repair

Use Resin Repair Kit or Liquid Epoxy Resin Repair Kit, PN 1051906.

All structural damage should have the damaged area reinforced with a backside layup patch. In many cases, access to the back of the damaged area is impossible. However, here are instructions for those easy-to-reach areas, with the instructions for hard-to-reach areas following.

1. Prepare the underside by grinding or sanding away all dirt, mud, tar, etc., and rough-sand the area. Bevel the opening but be certain to leave it rough for proper adhesion of the repair patch.

2. Cut the fiberglass cloth to size, making certain the patches are three inches larger than the opening. A minimum of five layers is necessary for an average job. Areas of high stress could require more strength.

3. Mix the resin and hardener or the epoxy-resin and hardener four parts resin to one part hardener. With the Resin Repair Kit can be found Thixatrope; add this to reduce the "runniness" of the material.

4. Saturate one layer of glass cloth with the mixture and lay it up underneath the damaged area. Smooth out any wrinkles and make certain the patch retains the original body contour.

5. Add successive layers of fiberglass cloth saturated with resin until the desired thickness is obtained. Try to remove all air bubbles between layers as you proceed.

6. Cure backing patch with heat lamp, if possible, for 15 to 20 minutes; place the lamp at least 12 inches away from the wet fiberglass. If a heat lamp is not available, air drying will require at least eight to ten hours.

7. Once the structural repair has been made from the back, the front may be treated as a cosmetic repair problem using solder to fill in the depression. Follow cosmetic repair steps 4 through 8.

Problems occur when the damaged area is difficult to reach from the rear—such as a door or a rear panel, for example. A backing patch is still required to complete the job properly and here's how to do it. You actually begin by making it on the front or top side of the car.

1. Trim the hole so that it is oval in shape with greater length than width.

2. Sand or grind the area so it has a V-shape at the edges and scuff-sand underneath in order that the patch will adhere when applied.

3. Cut from a piece of polyethylene plastic a segment seven to eight inches larger than the area to be repaired. Tape it down taut to the body so that it eliminates any air bubbles or pockets.

4. Again, apply at least five patches over the hole, being certain to thoroughly saturate each patch and remove all air bubbles and wrinkles. Don't press too hard and rupture the underlying plastic sheet.

5. Cure with heat lamp according to previous instructions.

6. When the patch has set up and cured, trim it to an oval shape making certain that it remains larger than the damaged area. It should have at least a one-inch overlap.

7. Drill two holes in the patch and run a wire through both holes so that you can grasp both ends on the same side of the patch.

8. Prior to applying the adhesive solder, insert the patch through the oval damaged area and pull up taut. If a good fit occurs, remove and apply the plastic or epoxy solder and reinsert.

9. Pull the patch up taut with the two wires tightly to ensure the spreading of the solder.

10. Run the wires around a dowel and twist, like a tourniquet, to maintain pressure while the soldered patch cures.

11. After the patch is cured, simply cut the wire and remove it from the patch.

12. Finish the structural repair in the manner outlined in 7 of the above section.

EQUIPMENT SELECTION FOR REFINISHING

The first and often the most singular impression made by a car—indeed, the one that usually makes a car "successful" or not—is that made by the paint job. Nothing else comes close to creating that impression; and if the finish is faded or dull, repainted and full of orange peel, runs, overspray and other problems, the car just won't stand up to its fullest expectations.

Refinishing a car is often time-consuming, repetitious, and back-breaking labor, but it definitely pays off in the end. Here are a few hints on how to repair and refinish your Corvette the right way.

Your first decision is whether to purchase or rent the tools necessary to refinish your car—power body working tools, air compressor, paint spray outfit, buffer, etc. If you live in a metropolitan area, professional-quality tools should be available at fairly reasonable prices. If you don't, however, you are going to have to borrow or purchase what you need. A Binks Model 18, "the finest spray gun available," is not necessary when a model from Sears will work just as well for your application.

The first piece of equipment to choose is the spray gun since this choice influences the size of air line, and, ultimately, the size of the air compressor required to supply that gun with the proper amount of air.

Several types of guns are available. External mix guns mix and atomize the air and fluid outside the air cap. This is the most common type of spray gun found in automotive work and it is the only type suitable for today's fast-drying paints such as acrylic lacquers. Internal mix guns, as their name implies, mix the air and paint inside the paint cup; they are used where low air pressures and slow-drying paints are used (Fig. 6-2).

Spray guns are further divided into suction and pressure feed models. The suction feed gun operates as a stream of compressed air passes through the gun, creating a vacuum that forces the paint out of the paint cup to the spray head. Here it is mixed with the compressed air, creating the spray pattern. The pressure gun has an air cap not designed to create a vacuum. The paint in the cup is forced to the spray head by air pressure from the compressor.

The choice of paint gun is critical because it influences the

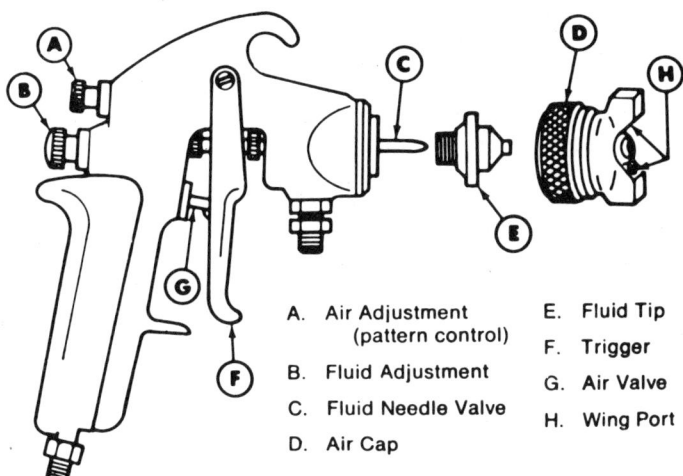

Fig. 6-2. All good conventional spray guns have the same basic components. Note A and B; these two knobs control paint pattern and density.

choice of compressor as it determines the amount of air required. Table 6-1 lists some of the spray guns offered by two of the top painting equipment manufacturers in the country. Notice that the top-of-the-line spray guns require a pressure of 50 psi (pounds per square inch) at a rate of at least 11 to 12 cfm (cubic feet per minute).

Compounding this problem is the fact that the air pressure drops the farther away from the compressor the spray gun is operated. This is due to the friction of the air as it passes through the line. As the length of the line increases, so does this pressure loss;

Table 6-1. Requirements for Selected Spray Guns.

Manufacturer	Cubic Feet/Minute	Air Pressure
Binks		
Model 7	11.5	50
18,62,69	11.4	50
15,26	4.6	50
DeVilbiss		
Model JGS-572-43EX	12.2	50
MBC-510-43EX	12.2	50
MGA-510-51E	6.7	40

201

in addition, the size of the line also influences this pressure loss. These factors are shown in Table 6-2.

Air compressors are available in many sizes and styles. The most popular type of compressor for automotive spray painting is the piston-type. Single or dual pistons units can provide working pressures of up to 200 psi and approximately 4 cfm for each rated horsepower of the compressor motor. Finding out what size you require for your needs isn't all that difficult. Here's an example:

Our selection for the spray gun is the DeVilbiss MGA-510-51E. DeVilbiss states that this is a full-size production gun at a moderate price able to handle lacquers, enamels, acrylics, primers, etc., at a working pressure of 50 psi using 7.7 cfm with a ¼-inch air hose. Next we have to decide on a hose length; we figure that 25 feet should provide us with enough room to work around the entire car with little problem.

A 25-foot, ¼-inch hose at 50 psi reduces air pressure by 16 pounds. This means that our compressor has to maintain 65 psi at the tank to produce 50 psi at the spray gun. Table 6-3 indicates that we can use the 80-pound cut-in, 100-pound cut-out section. Under continuous operation such as painting, 7.7 cfm will require an air compressor with a three-horsepower motor, although it is possible to get by with a two-horsepower motor since the requirement is on the borderline.

Two additional pieces of equipment should be mentioned. As the air is compressed, it heats up rapidly, the temperature of the heated, compressed air reaching from 150° to 500° F. As this air

Table 6-2. Air Pressure Loss at Spray Gun.

Air Hose Inside Diameter	10-Foot Length	15-Foot Length	25-Foot Length	50-Foot Length
¼-inch				
With 40# pressure	8	9½	12¾	24
With 50# pressure	10	12	16	28
With 60# pressure	12½	14½	19	31
With 70# pressure	14½	17	22½	34
With 80# pressure	16½	19½	25½	37
With 90# pressure	18¾	22	29	39½
5/16-inch				
With 40# pressure	2¾	3¼	4	8½
With 50# pressure	3½	4	5	10
With 60# pressure	4½	5	6	11½
With 70# pressure	5¼	6	7¼	13
With 80# pressure	6¼	7	8¾	14½
With 90# pressure	7½	8½	10½	16

Table 6-3. Air Compressor Horsepower Requirements.

Compressor Pressure		Air Consumption Cubic Feet/Minute Intermittent Operation	Air Consumption Cubic Feet/Minute Continuous Operation	hp
Cut In	Cut Out	Up to 3.5	Up to 1.2	1/3
		3.6 to 6.6	1.3 to 2.1	1/2
		6.7 to 10.5	2.2 to 2.8	3/4
		10.6 to 13.6	2.9 to 4.1	1
80	100	13.7 to 20.3	4.2 to 6.0	1 1/2
		20.4 to 26.6	6.1 to 7.4	2
		26.7 to 39.5	7.5 to 14.0	3
		39.6 to 58.0	14.1 to 21.5	5
		Up to 9.0	Up to 3.2	3/4
		9.1 to 12.0	3.3 to 4.0	1
		12.1 to 15.6	4.1 to 5.2	1 1/2
140	175	15.7 to 21.0	5.3 to 7.0	2
		21.1 to 33.0	7.1 to 11.0	3
		33.1 to 46.4	11.1 to 18.3	5

cools, it produces a potential problem—moisture. One of the most effective methods of dealing with this problem is the addition of an oil and water extractor (air drier). Many of these are also combined with an air regulator, which enables the cfm output to be adjusted.

The best location for the air drier would be after an initial run of 25 feet of hose, followed by an additional 25-foot section and ending with the spray gun. However, many of the smaller compressor units utilize only a single 25-foot section and the best location for this setup is directly at the outlet on the compressor.

The final piece of equipment needed is the air respirator with a replaceable filter. This should already have been in use during the body preparation, sanding, and grinding, and should not be a stranger. It is imperative to keep paint overspray and mist out of your lungs—not to mention all of that fiberglass dust.

PAINTING METHODS AND TECHNIQUES

Prior to running down to the auto parts store for a gallon or two of Roman Red paint, a number of questions must first be asked. For example, what type of color coat should be used (acrylic lacquer, Imron, nitrocellulose lacquer, acrylic enamel); which primer compliments which color coat; is a primer/sealer required;. is it necessary to remove all of the paint, etc.?

Before any of these questions can be answered, the initial problem of deciding what color to paint the car and what type of paint to use must be decided. Now, for most of us, the color shouldn't be too difficult a choice since it will probably be a color scheme as close to the original as possible. Determining the *type* of paint to use can be much more difficult. See Table 6-4.

Early Corvettes—1953 to 1957—were originally painted with nitrocellulose lacquers, although some 1957 finishes did not use this old-style paint. From 1958 to the present the paint used has been acrylic lacquer. From the standpoint of the Corvette restorer, only these two paints should ever be used

A brief mention of Imron and similar paints should be made. These polyurethane enamels have gained widespread acceptance since their introduction a few years back. Their chief claim is chemical, impact, and corrosion resistance. These paints are virtually indestructible. They clean up well and have amazing gloss retention. Their drawback, as far as Corvettes go, is that the colors are not correct and the paint is an enamel as compared to original lacquer. However, you are in luck if your car is black or you are going to paint frame and suspension components. Imron black appears to be very close to the original black used on Corvettes, although some say it appears to be a little too shiny.

That availability of paints also influences the choice. Most

Table 6-4. Color Coat Paint Application.

Covering Paint Over Base Paint	Recommendation	Reason
Lacquer over Lacquer	Yes	Thinner in the new paint will partly dissolve old paint so it blends well. Spot repairs work well, also.
Acrylic over Lacquer	No	Acrylic paint will crack on this sub-surface due to weathering even with a sealer over the lacquer.
Acrylic Lacquer over Acrylic Lacquer	Yes	Works well because it matches the original paint and has the same durability of original paint. Good for spot repairs.
Enamel over Lacquer	Complete Paint Job	Enamel will not blend in with lacquer.
Enamel over Acrylic Lacquer	Complete Paint Job	"
Lacquer over Acrylic Lacquer	No	Lacquer does not have the same durability of acrylic lacquer and the difference will become apparent over time.

Table 6-5. Cross Reference Paint Chart for 1953-1957 Corvettes.

Year	Color	Older DAL Prefix	Ditzler Acrylic Offset DDL Prefix
1953-57	Sportsman Red	70418	70966
	Polo White	8011	0829
	Shoreline Beige	21054	23620
	Pennant Blue	11238	13552
	Autumn Bronze	21151	22819
1955	Corvette Copper	21207	23393**
	Harvest Gold	80739	82171
	Gypsy Red	70575	71903
	Woodland Green	41318	44413
1956-57	Aztec Copper	21295	21927
	Cascade Green	41973	2561
	Arctic Blue	11537	13150
	Venetian Red	70694	71708

**This offset color is not red enough, too golden brown.

automotive paint manufacturers do not make nitrocellulose lacquer anymore. That's not to say it isn't available, although it will involve some homework. A limited number of advertisers in Hemming's and Old Cars Weekly newspaper sell nitro lacquer color-coat paint and corresponding primers.

Almost all major paint manufacturers can, although, supply you with an offset color, in acrylic, to match the nitrocellulose paint found on older Corvettes (Table 6-5). Since this is a different type of paint, the colors may not always duplicate the original color found on your car. This is especially true if you are only painting one panel or segment of the car. The original paint is bound to be faded and the new color, although, correct, won't match. Here's where an experienced hand at paint mixing and blending is required.

Paint manufacturers also supply replacement paint to match original colors on the remainder of Corvettes using acrylic lacquers. Table 6-6 indicates the availability of paint for second generation Corvettes, 1963-67, from three of the major paint companies. This is a complete cross-listing of all paints except for the Rinshed-Mason equivalent for 1963 Corvette Sebring White.

Before discussing how to proceed with repainting your Corvette, let's take a look at exactly how Chevrolet painted a Corvette. This information is condensed from the *1965 Chevrolet Corvette Specifications* book.

☐ Step One: Application of red primer.
☐ Step Two: Application of gray primer.

☐ Step Three: Corvette baked in drying oven.
☐ Step Four: Corvette wet-sanded, grey primer mostly removed with red primer acting as depth indicator.

Table 6-6. Cross Reference Paint Chart for 1963-1967 Corvettes.

Year	Code	Color Name	Ditzler	R-M	DuPont
1963	900	Tuxedo Black	DDL-9300	A-946	88-L
	912	Silver Blue	DDL-12546	A-1481	4250-L
	916	Daytona Blue	DDL-12696	A-1539	4395-L
	923	Riverside Red	DDL-70961	A-1138	2931-L
	932	Saddle Tan	DDL-22269	A-1537	4392-L
	936	Ermine White	DDL-8259	A-1199	4024-L
	941	Sebring White	DDL-32312		867-96417
1964	900	Tuxedo Black	DDL-9300	A-946	88-L
	912	Silver Blue	DDL-12546	A-1481	4250-L
	916	Daytona Blue	DDL-12696	A-1539	4395-L
	923	Riverside Red	DDL-70961	A-1138	2931-L
	932	Saddle Tan	DDL-22269	A-1537	4392-L
	936	Ermine White	DDL-8259	A-1199	4024-L
	940	Satin Silver	DDL-32173	A-1477	4247-L
1965	AA	Tuxedo Black	DDL-9300	A-946	88-L
	CC	Ermine White	DDL-8259	A-1199	4024-L
	FF	Nassau Blue	DDL-13057	A-1747	4690-L
	GG	Glen Green	DDL-43412	A-1745	4691-L
	MM	Milano Maroon	DDL-50706	A-1746	4689-L
	QQ	Silver Pearl	DDL-32449	A-1708	4621-L
	UU	Rally Red	DDL-71491	A-1744	4688-L
	XX	Goldwood Yellow	DDL-81450	A-1612	4530-L
1966	900	Tuxedo Black	DDL-9300	A-946	88-L
	972	Ermine White	DDL-8259	A-1199	4024-L
	974	Rally Red	DDL-71491	A-1744	4688-L
	976	Nassau Blue	DDL-13057	A-1747	4690-L
	978	Laguna Blue	DDL-13188	A-1826	4710-L
	980	Trophy Blue	DDL-13199	A-1825	4712-L
	982	Mosport Green	DDL-43535	A-1827	4713-L
	984	Sunfire Yellow	DDL-81540	A-1828	4711-L
	986	Silver Pearl	DDL-32449	A-1708	4621-L
	988	Milano Maroon	DDL-50706	A-1746	4689-L
1967	900	Tuxedo Black	DDL-9300	A-946	88-L
	972	Ermine White	DDL-8259	A-1199	4024-L
	974	Rally Red	DDL-71491	A-1744	4688-L
	976	Marina Blue	DDL-13364	A-1920	4850-L
	977	Lynndale Blue	DDL-13348	A-1912	4833-L
	980	Elkhart Blue	DDL-13347	A-1911	4834-L
	983	Goodwood Green	DDL-43652	A-1913	4835-L
	984	Sunfire Yellow	DDL-81540	A-1828	4711-L
	986	Silver Pearl	DDL-32449	A-1708	4621-L
	988	Marlboro Maroon	DDL-71584	A-1914	4836-L

☐ Step Five: Application of sealer.
☐ Step Six: Application of first color coat.
☐ Step Seven: Corvette baked in drying oven.
☐ Step Eight: Corvette dry-sanded.
☐ Step Nine: Application of three acrylic lacquer color coats.
☐ Step Ten: Corvette baked in drying oven twice.
☐ Step Eleven: Final oil sanding and polishing.

It is apparent that it is going to be extremely difficult to duplicate the steps taken by Chevrolet in its painting process. However, it is not really necessary to follow their steps to achieve equal or superior results. The real key to producing an outstanding paint job is patience and attention to detail.

Surface Preparation

Durability and overall appearance of any paint job depends on the condition of the surface to which the paint is applied. Assuming all preparatory bodywork has been completed, this is the time to either featheredge all repaired areas into the surrounding paint or completely strip all paint from the body.

Several commercial paint strippers are available at auto paint stores. Basically, you use them like this: First remove all chrome and accessory trim, brush on a medium-to-thick coat of stripper and allow to stand for about 15 minutes, then scrape lifted paint off with a *plastic* scraper (a putty knife or metal scraper can easily gouge fiberglass and therefore are not recommended).

Wash the car with soap and water, making certain that all of the soap is removed from the car. Apply a good wax and silicone remover next to eliminate any grease or wax buildup on the body. Two types are available but only one is suitable for Corvettes. Typical wax and grease/silicone removers are designed to work at a slow, evaporative pace. The problem with this is that it could possibly work its way into the fiberglass before evaporating, only to be trapped by the primer and surface later.

The best choice for removing residual wax and grease is an enamel reducer. This product will do the same job as the typical degreaser but will evaporate rapidly. Wipe the reducer on with a clean cloth, doing a panel at a time. Wipe it off with an absolutely lint-free towel. Complete the process by blowing the surface dry and going over the entire car with a tack rag.

Masking

Unless the body is to be completely painted and all chrome and trim components are removed, these areas must be covered up with masking tape and paper. If the job is done carelessly, some of the paint will be removed as the tape and paper is removed. If possible, remove the part rather than mask it.

Begin by placing masking tape around the windshield chrome. Press it into place and proceed around the frame. If applicable, do the same to the rear window. Now tape paper to the existing taped windshield frame to mask off the window. Don't try to combine these two operations.

Mask off the remaining areas in a similar fashion. Headlights, taillights, side chrome, etc., should be completely covered. To protect tires and wheels, cover them with plastic garbage bags.

Mixing the Paint

Paint supplied for automotive use must be diluted before use. Thinner is designed to be used with lacquer paint; reducer is used with enamel paint. Since we have decided to concentrate on acrylic paint, only thinner need be discussed.

Since thinner is designed to help the paint flow out to maximum effectiveness, several types are available from each paint manufacturer. The difference between the thinners is the air temperature application, although some are only for color coats. Table 6-7 shows the thinners offered by Martin-Senour Paints. The recommended temperature is the ambient air temperature of the paint spray area. Remember, if you bring a car inside to the spray area from outside and a temperature difference exists, allow the car to come to room temperature. Use of the wrong thinner can cause poor flow, poor gloss, improper drying, flaking, peeling, dry spray, etc.

The thinner is added after the paint is mixed. The paint must be mixed thoroughly in order to achieve the correct color. Begin by stirring with a paint paddle, making certain to reach the bottom of the can. Next, pour the paint back and forth from one can to another, add a small amount of thinner to dissolve any residue left in the bottom of the original paint can, and pour back and forth a few more times. Reduce the paint according to the directions on the label with

Table 6-7. Martin Senour Acrylic Lacquer Thinners.

No.	Name	Speed	Application	Temp.
3092	Acrylic Lacquer Thinner	Fastest Dry	Color & Undercoats	60 –80 F.
3094	Acrylic Lacquer Thinner	Very Slow	Color Only	80 –95 F.
3095	Twin Thin	Slow Dry	Color Only	75 –90 F.
3099	Acrylic Lacquer Thinner	Medium Dry	Color & Undercoats	70 –85 F.

the proper amount of thinner. As you are pouring the paint from can to can, use a high-quality automotive paint filter.

Primer and Color Coat Application

With the paint mixed and the spray gun hooked up to the compressor, it's time to adjust the spray gun for the proper spray pattern and density. Refer back to illustration 6-2 and note the position of the air adjustment and fluid adjustment knobs. It is important to have the correct spray pattern, one that resembles an elongated ellipse with an even, uniform distribution of paint. Too narrow a spray pattern will concentrate the paint into a small area; too large a spray pattern will cause excessive overspray and a dry, rough surface.

Once the proper spray pattern is established, actual painting may begin. To achieve the proper stroke, the pass should begin *before* the area you intend to paint and stop *after* the intended area is covered. Strokes should go first in one direction and then return the opposite way, with each stroke overlapping the previous one by 50 percent. Make certain the gun is not tilted away from the surface or turned from side-to-side. Either of these movements will cause uneven coverage.

Once the equipment is ready to proceed, the next step is application of the primer coat. The first coat should be applied lightly and allowed to flash-dry for about 35 to 45 minutes. Extra coats may be applied with usually three to four coats being sufficient. When the primer has dried thoroughly, apply a thin dust coat of primer in a contrasting color. This will enable you to check for waves and minor surface imperfections. Wait at least two to four hours after the last coat of primer and block-sand with #280-grit wet sandpaper.

If the car's surface is free from defects, apply two more coats of primer and let the paint dry 18 to 24 hours. Block-sand the entire car again with #400-grit paper. Blow the car dry and wipe with a tack rag.

Before the color coat comes an important step. Apply an all-purpose sealer designed to be used with the brand of paint you are using. This will promote better paint adhesion and chemical bonding and prevent any chance of sand-scratch swelling. If you wait longer than one hour from application of the sealer to application of the first color coat, the sealer must be scuff-sanded with #600-grit sandpaper, wet or dry.

Color coats are applied next. It is best to first test the color by applying paint to a test card. Do this regardless of whether you are just blending in a spot repair or refinishing the entire car. It's good to see *exactly* what color you are going to apply! Use a piece of thin cardboard, preferably of the type used by laundries. Tape the cardboard to a vertical surface and make your test passes. If the card does not produce the color desired, several alterations are possible. If the color is too dark, adjust the fluid feed so less paint flows out or increase the fan adjustment to get a wider spray pattern. To darken the color, reverse one or both of these steps.

Metallics are among the more difficult paint types to apply. Metallic paint contains small flakes of metal suspended in a paint medium. The metal particles reflect incoming light; the overall effect is determined by the manner in which the paint is applied. Metallic paint applied wet allows the metallic pieces time to settle parallel to the car's surface and appears darker in color due to the uniform reflection of light. Non-uniform reflection is caused by a "dry" application of paint; this will dry very rapidly after application, causing the metallic pieces to become trapped in a random array and appearing much brighter in color.

If you are painting an entire car, you can decide which metallic paint appearance is most desirable. The problem lies with matching metallic paint for a spot repair. This paint matching is a most difficult problem and requires much patience.

COLOR SANDING AND COMPOUNDING

After all the color coats have been applied, the final color coat can to brought up to its full luster by color sanding and compounding. This process is nothing more than sanding the car with superfine sandpaper and then buffing with a polishing compound. Begin with #600-grit wet sandpaper and *lots* of water. The purpose of this is to remove overspray, dust, and orange peel, resulting in a clean, smooth finish. Wet the surface and continue to add water as you sand. Check the surface frequently; when it is smooth, move to another area. When sanding is completed, rinse the sludge from the car and dry. Don't be concerned if the surface appears dull; compounding will remove this temporary appearance.

Compounding is accomplished by either hand or machine. Hand-applied compound is coarser than machine-applied compound and is applied with a damp rag in straight back-and-forth strokes, not in a circular motion. It may be buffed by either hand or machine.

Machine-applied compound is finer and should be thinned with water to the consistency of a cream before application. Apply dabs to a small area and run the buffing machine in straight lines. *Don't* use the buffing machine on ridges; do them by hand after the panel has been worked with the buffer. *Note*: Compound nitrocellulose lacquers at speeds up to 1200 rpm and acrylic lacquers at speeds up to 3000 rpm. Be careful of leaving the buffing machine in one spot too long and burning through the new paint!

SOFT BUMPER REFINISHING

In addition to the normal painting supplies required, a special primer and paint additive will be necessary for the soft bumpers. Instructions for painting these areas are as follows:
1. Wash bumper with wax and silicone remover.
2. Scuff-sand with #320-grit sandpaper.
3. Apply two coats of primer specifically designed for soft plastic bumper application. Dry thoroughly.
4. Wet sand with #400-grit or #500-grit paper.
5. Add proper flexible agent for the paint used to the paint.
6. Reduce the mixture according to the label directions.
7. Apply color coats until desired color is obtained.
8. Color sand and compound as previously detailed.

REFINISHING PROBLEMS

Bleeding: Surface discolors after painting.
    Cause: Solvent from new paint penetrates old paint, releasing dye which comes to surface, usually reds and maroons.
    Remedy: Remove all color coats, apply sealer and repaint.

Blistering: Paint bubbles broken or flattened, lack of gloss if bubbles are minute.
    Cause: Painting over silicone, wax, or grease; exposure to humidity or moisture in spray line.
    Remedy: Remove paint, prepare surface properly, eliminate moisture from air lines.

Blushing: Surface finish becomes milky appearing.
    Cause: Thinner too fast for temperature or high humidity.
    Remedy: Use a retarder when spraying on humid days to thin the spray.

Chalking: Lack of gloss and powdery surface.
    Cause: Natural weathering of paint, insufficient agitation of paint.

Remedy: Sand to remove surface layer paint, refinish.

Checking, crazing, cracking: Irregular, crowfoot separations.
    Cause: Incompatible brands of paint products, insufficient drying time between coats, or ingredients not mixed thoroughly.
    Remedy: Remove paint through damaged area and repaint.

Cratering: Small holes throughout the surface.
    Cause: Identical to blisters but not broken.
    Remedy: Identical to blistering.

Dull finish: Surface appears dull, lusterless.
    Cause: Washing with caustic cleaners, compounding before thinner in topcoat evaporated, topcoats applied on wet subcoats.
    Remedy: Make certain finish has dried and treat with mild rubbing compound.

Fisheyes: Raising or swelling of wet film or peeling when dry. Resembles small, circular "fish eyes."
    Cause: Contamination on old surface.
    Remedy: Apply commercial fish eye eliminator over affected area. Remove finish and repaint, if necessary.

Lifting: Finish swells and raises while setting up.
    Cause: Surface not cleaned properly, improper drying of previous coat, applying acrylic lacquer over uncured air dry enamel.
    Remedy: Remove finish and repaint.

Orange peel: Surface resembles the skin of an orange.
    Cause: Surface drying too fast, improper air pressure, improper paint flow, thinner mixture wrong ratio or wrong type.
    Remedy: Enamel—Apply mild polishing compound until surface is smooth. Lacquer—Sand with #-grit paper and refinish.

Peeling: Paint separates, breaks and peels from surface.
    Cause: Improper cleaning of subsurface, wrong undercoat,

paint application on cold surface, incompatible paint products.
Remedy: Remove damaged paint and repaint.

Runs and Sags: Mass of paint slipping on wet film.
Cause: Too much air pressure, holding gun too close to car, improper gun adjustment, improper reduction of paint.
Remedy: Wipe off immediately or allow to dry thoroughly, remove and repaint.

Sand Scratches: Coarse gouges in surface showing through topcoat.
Cause: Improper cleaning and preparation of surface, undercoat applied too heavy, wrong or poor quality thinner or swelling of topcoat solvents.
Remedy: Remove paint, resand smooth, apply primer sealer and repaint.

Waterspotting: Mass of spots appearing in color coats.
Cause: Exposure of finish to rain or moisture before paint is thoroughly dry.
Remedy: Compound to remove spots, if necessary, sand and repaint.

Wrinkling: Topcoat wrinkles and puckers like a prune.
Cause: Excessive paint film thickness, improper enamel reducer, application under excessively hot and humid conditions, improper lacquer thinner.
Remedy: Remove wrinkled paint and refinish.

Index

A

Adjustments, fuel injection, 141-147
Aerovette, 27
Air cleaner, fuel injection, 142
Air meter, 134-136, 149-150, 151-152
A. O. Smith Corporation, 19
Arkus-Duntov, Zora, 8-10, 15, 17, 20, 21, 26, 167
Astro II, 26

B

Bleeding, 211
Blistering, 211
Blushing, 211
Body removal, 181-182
Brake, parking, 172
Brakes, disc, 167-172
Brown, Arnold R., 167

C

Caliper replacement, 169-171
Carpeting, 191
CERV-1, 17
Chalking, 211-212,
Chassis disassembly, 184-188
Checking, 212
Choke valve, 150-151
Cobra, 18
Cold enrichment, 143
Cole, Ed, 2, 4, 8, 15, 26
Color coat, 209-210
Color sanding, 210-211
Compensator, hot idle, 140-141

Compounding, 210-211
Control arm, 156-158
Corvette, 1953, 37-39
Corvette, 1954, 40-42
Corvette, 1955, 43-44
Corvette, 1956, 45-47
Corvette, 1957, 48-50
Corvette, 1958, 51-53
Corvette, 1959, 54-56
Corvette, 1960, 57-59
Corvette, 1961, 60-62
Corvette, 1962, 63-65
Corvette, 1963, 66-69
Corvette, 1964, 70-72
Corvette, 1965, 73-75
Corvette, 1966, 76-79
Corvette, 1967, 80-83
Corvette, 1968, 84-86
Corvette, 1969, 87-89
Corvette, 1970, 90-92
Corvette, 1971, 93-95
Corvette, 1972, 96-98
Corvette, 1973, 99-101
Corvette, 1974, 102-104
Corvette, 1975, 105-107
Corvette, 1976, 108-110
Corvette, 1977, 111-113
Corvette, 1978, 114-116
Corvette, 1979, 117-119
Corvette, 1980, 120-122
Corvette, 1981, 123-126
Corvette, 1982, 127-129
Corvette, 1984, 131-133

Corvette Gran Sport, 18
Corvette SS, 13-14
Cosmetic repair, fiberglass, 197-198
Cracking, 212
Cratering, 212
Crazing, 212
Curtice, Harlow, 2

D

Daytona Beach Speed Week, 10
Dermatitis, 194
Dull finish, 212

E

Earl, Harley, 2, 12
Economy stop, 145-146
Electronic control module, 166
Engine removal, 182-184
Enrichment diaphragm, 153-154
Estes, "Pete", 20

F

Fast idle, 143
Ferrari 308 GTB, 27
Fessenden, F. J., 5
Fiberglass refinishing, 200-203
Fiberglass repair, 193-200
Fisher Body Division, 4
Fisheyes, 212
Ford Cobra, 18
Ford, R. G., 5
Ford Thunderbird, 8
Fuel control system, 137
Fuel filter, 141-142
Fuel injection systems, 134-166
Fuel meter, 137, 152-153

Glasspan Company, 1-2
Goldsmith, Paul, 11
Gormeson, Elmer, 4

H

Harrison Radiator, 28
High pressure pump, 158-160
Holls, David, 20

I

Idle air, 136
Idle circuit, 140
Idle speed, 142-143
Injection, throttle body, 163-166
Intake manifold, 160-161

J

Jakust, Carl, 4
Jonas, H. George, 169

Jordan, Chuck, 27

K

Kaiser, Henry, 1
Keating, Thomas H., 2
Kirksite dies, 4
Kleiber, Tony, 5

L

Lifting, paint, 212
Lund, Robert D., 24
Lunn Laminate Company, 5

M

Main control diaphragm, 154-155
Maintenence, fuel injection, 141-147
Main venturi signal, 136
Mako Shark, 19-20
Manometer, 144-145
Masking, 207-208
McLean, Robert F., 2
McLellan, Dave, 27, 31
Methodology, restoration, 174-179
Mitchell, William, 12, 15, 20, 26-27
Mitchell-Bentley Corporation, 19
Molded Fiber Glass Company, 4-5, 19, 195
Morrison, Robert S., 4-5, 195-196
Motorama Auto Show, 1, 2-4

N

Nassau Trophy Race, 11
National Corvette Restorer's Society, 179
Nozzles, 162

O

Official Pace Car, 24
Olley, Maurice, 2
Orange peel, 212
Owen-Corning, 1

P

Paint, duplicating, 204-205
Paint, mixing, 208-209
Painting, 203-213
Palmer, Jerry, 25-28
Parking brake, 172
Parts, restoration, 177-179
Peeling, 212-213
Power stop, 146-147
Premo, Jim, 4
Primer, 209-210
Problems, refinishing, 211-213

R

Ratio lever, 144

Reassembly, Corvette, 191-192
Refinishing, fiberglass, 200-203
Refinishing problems, 211-213
Refinishing, soft bumper, 211
Regulator, 203
Repainting, 203-213
Repair kits, fiberglass, 196-197
Restoration, Corvette, 173-192
Rondine, 15
Rotor, disc brake, 171-172
Runs, 213
Rybicki, Irv, 27

S

Sags, 213
Sanding, color, 210-211
Sanding scratches, 213
Schaafsma, Fred, 32
Scratches, sanding, 213
Service, fuel injection, 147-162
Shark XP-755, 14-15
Sheet molding compound (SMC), 196
Shelby, Carrol, 18
Shenkel, Max, 29
Shinoda, Larry, 20
Silver Anniversary Corvette, 24
Soft bumper refinishing, 211

Spill valve, 155
Spray equipment, 200-203
Starting system, 139
Structural repair, fiberglass, 198-200
Surface preparation, 207

T

Thinners, 208-209
Thompson, Dick, 14
Throttle body injection, 163-166
Throttle valve, 151
Tools, restoration, 174-177
Transmission removal, 182-184
Tritt, Bill, 1-2

W

Waterspotting, 213
Wobble pump, high pressure, 137
Wrinkling, 213

X

XP-700, 12, 13
XP-755, 14-15
XP-819, 26
XP-882, 23, 26
XP-895, 26
XP-987GT, 23 26

OTHER POPULAR TAB BOOKS OF INTEREST

Basic Body Repair & Refinishing for the Weekend Mechanic (No. 2122—$13.50 paper)
Convertibles: The Complete Story (No. 2110—$20.50 paper)
Car Design: Structure & Architecture (No. 2104—$20.50 paper)
Car Interior Restoration—3rd Edition (No. 2102—$7.25 paper)
All About Electric & Hybrid Cars (No. 2097—$9.95 paper; $16.95 hard)
Supertuning Your Firebird Trans-Am (No. 2088—$9.95 paper)
The New Mazda Guide (No. 2082—$13.50 paper)
The 1960s Supercars: A Repair and Restoration Guide (No. 2077—$13.50 paper)
The Complete Handbook of Automotive Power Trains (No. 2069—$9.95 paper)
Dreamboats & Milestones: Cars of the '50s (No. 2065—$11.95 paper; $18.95 hard)
Formula Vee/Super Vee—Racing, History, and Chassis/Engine Prep (No. 2063—$6.95 paper)
Boss Wheels—End of the Supercar Era (No. 2050—$7.95 paper; $9.95 hard)
The Ford Mustang—1964-1973 (No. 2048—$8.25 paper)
The Coach Trimmer's Art (No. 1213—$12.95 hard)
Vanner's How-To Guide to Murals, Painting & Pinstriping (No. 1032—$5.95 paper)
101 Vantastic Ideas To Improve Your Van (No. 1018—$4.95 paper)
How to Convert Your Car, Van, or Pickup to Diesel (No. 968—$7.95 paper)
Step-By-Step Guide to Brake Servicing (No. 818—$8.95 paper)
Step-By-Step Guide: Carburetor Tuneup & Overhaul (No. 814—$8.95 paper)

Customizing Your Van—2nd Edition (No. 2112—$11.50 paper; $16.95 hard)
The RV/Truck/Van Conversion Guide (No. 2109—$12.95 paper)
Propane Conversion of Cars, Trucks & RVs (No. 2103—$9.95 paper; $14.95 hard)
Automobile Restoration Guide—3rd Edition (No. 2101—$8.25 paper)
Choosing the Right Car for the 1980s (No. 2095—$10.25 paper)
Morgans: Pride of the British (No. 2083—$29.95 hard)
The Triumph Spitfire (No. 2079—$6.95 paper)
Troubleshooting Old Cars (No. 2075—$9.25 paper; $13.95 hard)
Rebuilding the Famous Ford Flathead (No. 2066—$7.25 paper; $9.95 hard)
Studebaker: The Complete Story (No. 2064—$39.95 hard)
The Complete MG Guide—Model by Model: 2nd Edition (No. 2056—$4.95 paper)
The Giant Book of 4 × 4's & Off-Road Vehicles (No. 2049—$10.95 paper)
Modern Diesel Cars (No. 2046—$7.95 paper; $9.95 hard)
The Complete Guide To Car Stereo Systems (No. 1121—$7.95 paper)
Automotive Air Conditioning Handbook—Installation, Maintenance & Repair (No. 1020—$9.25 paper)
Fixin' Up Your Van On a Budget (No. 982—$10.25 paper; $13.95 hard)
Do-It-Yourselfer's Guide to Auto Body Repair & Painting (No. 949—$7.95 paper; $10.95 hard)
How to Repair Diesel Engines (No. 817—$10.95 paper; $15.95 hard)

TAB TAB BOOKS Inc.
Blue Ridge Summit, Pa. 17214

Send for FREE TAB Catalog describing over 750 current titles in print.